THIS EARTH IS OURS

etter. When I was young, this commitment to values first led me to the non-profit world. I worked for years helping educate, advocate,

by businesses I worked with who would just do the things that I advocated for. I would strive to educate or change opinions, while a

ny MBA because I saw the possibility of business doing good for the planet. Nature's Path, and its vision of leaving the earth better, is

are all so values driven and passionate about leaving the earth better. I know I am lucky in my role here, and I am incredibly excited for

re's Path, a golden opportunity to help heal people and empower them towards optimum health by educating them on the importance

a day in your life.' At the end of the day, you have to feel good with what you do. There are many challenges in finding quality organic

d of our contribution to society and Mother Nature. —**Sofia** ¶ I was finishing up my Masters in Food and Resource Economics at UBC

es and ultimately was a business that cared about the environment. I had spent a lot of time researching the company and found that

vid gardener so local delicious food was part of my roots. Nature's Path could not be a more perfect fit—plus, I was also a consumer.

aving a book reading at Banyen books, five blocks from my house. I thought it would be the perfect opportunity to hear him speak and

school as an R&D Associate Food Scientist. I have been at Nature's Path now for two years and I am so grateful to have found a home

great people. What more could a girl ask for? —**Ellie** ¶ One of the things that most impressed me when I came to Nature's Path was

sued those things. As a company, we've made food for hungry people on the downtown East Side, we've patrolled local beaches and

sm, and spirituality. ¶ To me, Nature's Path is the logical extension of Arran and Ratana Stephens. It's what happens when enthusiasm

ting what I do from who I am. That's why Nature's Path is such a happy home for me—it's important for me to belong to a company

ined the Nature's Path team six years ago, on September 22, 2008. Since then, every day I go to my job very enthusiastic with a huge

Nature's Path cares for their employees and their personal development by offering activities such as meditation to nourish the soul,

d benefits such as the Get Fit program to keep us in good health. ¶ Second, Nature's Path's vision has encouraged me to find better

it, we can all contribute with small changes in our personal lives. I hope to be part of Nature's Path for many more years and be part

or to working at Nature's Path, I was working for a big box retail company where the focus was to get people to buy product they didn't

e about GMOs and the impact they have. We strive to do what we can to avoid them for our children. They have no choice in what they

e to work everyday knowing that as we convert and educate the public about organic and non-GMO food that they will be healthier and

eat pride in doing that. This inspires me to look for new sources and learn about new ingredients that we can add for the betterment of

g if I would be interested in helping out with the design of some granola bar boxes for him, I had never even heard of Nature's Path

ting went fine, and a week or so later I came back with some box designs that I thought nicely solved their design issues. My takeaway

vision, or the Nature's Path brand, and it's something I have been trying to make up for ever since. I must have gotten a bit better at,

bringing me into the fold, Arran, and hopefully I'm listening a bit better now. —**Jeff** ¶ I'm so happy I landed in such a safe, nurturing

d that here, within the mission of the company and the warmth of its people. I feel like my feet are now firmly 'on the path'! —**Suzanne**

995. I started at the head office when it was our only plant. The facility in Delta produced and shipped from that one site. We were so

r three. To look back now and see how small we were—and how large we have now become—is a huge accomplishment. I remember

f our export business. It truly was a family right from the start. I cannot believe it has been 19 years as it seems like yesterday.

THIS EARTH IS OURS

30 ORGANIC YEARS
ALONG NATURE'S PATH

Gurdeep Stephens

DEDICATION

This Earth is ours to have and hold
The dust beneath our feet
We have these hands to cherish it
To help the hungry eat
And if we treat it as our friend
Ten times it will repay
The sweat, the toil, our good red soil
This Earth is ours today

This Earth is ours to treat with love
Right here beneath our feet
I know that on the summer's dust
The steam of rain is sweet
And when we're weary, old and worn,
We'll know that we can say
We'll pass it on to other hands
This Earth is ours that day.

This song was written by my Grandpa Rupert on Goldstream Berry Paradise in the 1950s. Rupert worshipped Nature and said to my dad, Arran, "Always leave the soil better than you found it." This book is dedicated to the Earth. The Earth belongs to us all; may we be worthy stewards and shepherds. Organic agriculture sets out to mimic natural processes. May we continue in harmony with Nature through organic farming to purify the soils, water and air. May we honour and respect all creation, replenish the soil and leave the Earth better than when we arrived.

CONTENTS

A pollinator in Arran and Ratana's home garden.

Nature's Path was North America's first cereal company to be third-party certified organic and North America's second food processor to be certified organic. Our company has consistently been North America's #1 organic brand of cereal, but we can never rest upon our laurels. We have a great deal more to accomplish, from fighting for your right to know what's in your food to maintaining strong organic standards and increasing organic, non-toxic farmland as a bulwark against the tide of chemical pollution and global warming.

Thank you for your interest in our journey; it's been filled with fun, passion, success and failures, hard work and constant Earth honouring. We have remained independent rather than selling out; we wish the legacy of Nature's Path to continue for generations. We may have started alone on this journey, but we marveled each time as many gifted souls joined us to create something of enduring beauty and value to our world. As the poet Darshan Singh says,

I started alone on the journey of love
filled with faith and zeal;
at every step, travelers joined me
and soon we were a caravan.

Arran & Ratana

WELCOME

Let the beauty we love be what we do;
there are hundreds of ways to kneel and kiss the ground.

— RUMI

Thank you for being a loyal friend, team member, customer, influencer, supplier, inspiration and muncher of our organic cereals, bars and tortilla chips. We have been asked to tell our "story behind the story," so when our talented daughter Gurdeep offered to compile a history of the company, we were grateful to have memories preserved in print before they are lost to the winds of time. Although this book celebrates our 30 years as Nature's Path, it goes back many decades to our farm roots and the early businesses we started—not all successful, and some more so than others!

Arran and Ratana's garden.

FOREWORD

For most of human history, food was about survival. If you were alive 50,000 years ago, or in most of the world even 3,000 years ago, you ate what you could get ahold of that would keep your body going for another day. You probably died pretty young, but you also didn't have a high likelihood of coming down with a chronic disease. For most of human history, getting enough calories to survive was the fundamental purpose of food; and, tragically, for far too many people in the world today, it still is.

But in the last century, with the advent of global transportation mechanisms, the expansion of cropland productivity and the growth of consumer culture, the central organizing principle of food has become commerce. Modern supermarkets may stock more than 500 different kinds of breakfast cereals—far more than anyone could possibly need for mere survival. Many of us can now choose between eating "Chinese," "Italian," "Thai," "Mexican," or "Middle Eastern" food—all without having to leave our home town. We have a stunning array of flavours, textures and styles to choose from, and most of us can access food grown 6,000 miles away, and processed 2,000 miles away—at our local store. A vast network of enterprises are now in the business of growing and manufacturing foods for the lowest possible price, and then selling them to as many people as they can, for the highest possible profits.

Our modern food system is financially profitable for a few; but it is morally bankrupt for all of us.

From animals whose lives are the product of unspeakable cruelty, to farm workers who are exposed to so many pesticides and inhumane conditions that their average life expectancy is 49 years, to consumers who are beset by a toxic food system that is driving epidemic rates of disease, the reality is clear: Our modern food system is killing us.

The truth is that most of us are basing our diets on food-like products that are laced with chemicals, pesticides, hormones, antibiotics, genetically modified organisms and stunning amounts of added sugar. The average American now eats more than 150 pounds of added sugar each year, while less than 5 percent of our population is consuming the recommended amount of fiber.

Toxic food is contributing to epidemic rates of illness. You only have to look around to see the sad reality of the Standard American Diet. In the US, more than two-thirds of the population is now overweight or obese, and heart disease and stroke are killing more than 700,000 people every year. The National Institutes of Health reports that in the 1960s less than 2 percent of America's kids had a chronic health condition. Today it's over 25 percent. And one in three American children is expected to get diabetes.

Behind every one of these numbers is a human being who is suffering, and lives and loved ones that are being lost. It's deeply

View of the buffer zone between our organic Saskatchewan farm and our conventional neighbour.

personal for all of us. Who in your family has been impacted by diabetes, cancer, Alzheimer's or heart disease?

As you probably already know, all of these conditions are directly linked to lifestyle and food choices.

Survival and commerce are great and important. But if we're to survive as people, and perhaps even as a species, we have to upgrade our food operating system. If Food 1.0 was Survival, and Food 2.0 was Commerce, then perhaps it's time for Food 3.0: Health.

In Food 3.0, we make healthy people and a healthy planet the fundamental organizing principle of our food lives. We restore dignity and integrity to our food system. We treat animals and farm workers with respect. And in Food 3.0, healthy food, understood to be a basic human right, is affordable and available to everyone, of every ethnic and economic background.

Food 3.0 means vastly lower rates of chronic illness—which saves trillions of dollars in medical care—and a healthier and more capable population. Food 3.0 means a more sustainable and productive economy. There's plenty of money to be made in Food 3.0, and it's not at the expense of ethics, health or the future of our world.

Nature's Path, and the Stephens family, have been on the vanguard of standing for Food 3.0 for decades. Starting long before

John and Ocean Robbins.

it was "cool" to eat healthy, and long before most people even realized there was a link between diet and health, they've been steadily working to provide real, delicious alternatives for people who care about their bodies and their health.

Our family lived in British Columbia, Canada, in the 1970s. We grew most of our own food, and were doing our best to break away from the junk-food consumer culture, and to enjoy real, natural foods. At that time, there weren't many health food stores in the world. But there was one, in Vancouver, called LifeStream, that had been founded by Arran and Ratana

Stephens. LifeStream was something of a lifeline for us. We lived on Salt Spring Island, several hours ferry-ride away. But any time we could get to Vancouver, we'd excitedly look forward to the chance to shop at LifeStream. There we could find a practical treasure trove of delicious foods, including an abundance of organic fruits and vegetables.

At a time when healthy food was far from mainstream, Life-Stream was, for our family, a light in the food world.

In the decades that followed, generations of the Stephens family went on to found Nature's Path, and to build it into one of the world's most iconic organic brands. For decades they've been proving that it is possible to do well by making a difference, and that profits for a company can co-exist with high integrity and the wellbeing of the planet.

The Stephens started living Food 3.0 long before it was popular. And now they're helping push it ever-more into the mainstream.

As leaders in the movement for organic, natural, non-GMO, nutritious and sustainable food, we believe that this family is part of the hope of our world.

— JOHN ROBBINS, author, *Diet for a New America,* cofounder and President, the Food Revolution Network

— OCEAN ROBBINS, co-author, *Voices of the Food Revolution,* co-founder and CEO, the Food Revolution Network

ABOVE AND OPPOSITE: Pollinators at work in our gardens.

INTRODUCTION

Nature's Path started out as a one-product, one-man operation in the back of a restaurant. We have evolved into an inspiring organization employing hundreds of dedicated team members, with dynamic and diverse operations that include organic farm-land and state-of-the-art manufacturing facilities. People continually ask us, "How did this happen?" That is the story I want to tell you in this book.

I grew up in a hippie-infused countercultural world with parents who believed that putting healthy food into their bodies was the key to optimum health and spiritual well-being. I came of age alongside my parents' healthy food companies, from LifeStream to Woodlands to Nature's Path, starting as carrot-peeler. Today, in 2015, my parents manage the operations of Nature's Path along with my siblings, Jyoti and Arjan, and our amazing team. This distance from daily operations has granted me the broad perspective needed to write this history.

My grandfather Rupert Stephens was born in 1896 in England and raised on a farm in Canada. As an eager lad of 18, he enlisted as a captain in the Scottish Infantry to fight in the Great War. Rupert returned broken and rarely spoke of the war again, except to shudder and say, "War is a terrible thing."

This veteran found love in my grandmother Gwendolyn and took solace in the soil. Rupert was a handsome, gentle soul with a barrel chest. A dreamer and a hard worker, Rupert also wrote many songs in praise of the land. Gwen, his elegant "farm-wife," loved the feel of the soil in her hands and cherished Nature. Rupert grew berries first on Mountain Valley Farm near Duncan, on British Columbia's beautiful Vancouver Island, and then on the 80-acre Goldstream Berry Paradise near Victoria. A yellowed newspaper clipping from a family scrapbook calls Rupert's farm "a mecca for professional horticulturists and berry growers, commercial and amateur."

Rupert and Gwen's first son, Godfrey, was born in 1939. Five years later, in January 1944, Gwen was famously unloading sacks of potatoes from the back of a pickup truck when she gave birth to my father. Born in 1909 in Washington State, Gwen felt strong

LEFT TO RIGHT: Arran at christening, Arran age 6, berry stand at Goldstream Berry Paradise.

ties to her Scottish-English roots and named their son after the Isle of Arran, off the west coast of Scotland.

My family's history is inseparable from the development of the organic farming movement that sprouted in the 1940s. Until World War II, almost all agriculture was technically "organic," with little use of chemical fertilizers and pesticides. The Canadian organic agriculture movement was born in the 1940s and 1950s as a response to the burgeoning chemical fertilizer and pesticide industry.

Rupert was distrustful of these new methods of agriculture gaining vogue in the postwar years. He kept to kelp, manure, compost, mulch and sawdust and produced arguably the biggest, best and juiciest berries to be found, including his own new varieties, like the cross between blackberry and loganberry. According to Arran, with Grandpa Rupert's natural methods, he was achieving yields of over 10 tons of berries per acre from the Vancouver Island soil, much to the puzzlement and awe of his more conventional peers.

Looking back, we can see that Rupert was part of a growing movement in protest against chemical farming methods. The earliest organic agriculture experimenter and pioneer in the 20th century was Sir Albert Howard (1873–1947), author of the classic 1940 text on organic farming, *An Agricultural Testament*. Rudolph Steiner of Germany (1861–1925) founded Biodynamics, one of the first movements in sustainable agriculture, which included special herbal preparations for compost and planting

Gwen at the Goldstream berry stand, 1953.

Fruit Grown in Sawdust Creates Island Paradise

By C. V. FAULKNOR

ABOUT 11 miles out of Victoria, where the Island Highway poises for its drop into Goldstream Canyon, a song-writing berry-grower, Rupert Stevens, has applied his own special brand of magic to coarse, gravelly soil that was raw bushland only four years ago. The miracle-working genie was sawdust, used as a mulch, and the horticultural wonderland created became "Berry Paradise"—home of the Goldstream ever-bearing strawberry.

In Stephens' own words, "On my farm sawdust is the slave that saves me from hundreds of hours of weeding and cultivating. Shielded by a carpet of sawdust, millions of earthworms work for me the year around, safe from extremes of heat, drought, and frost."

CHOICE OF SITE

In choosing the site of Berry Paradise, location, rather than soil, was the deciding factor. Like a natural showcase the land rises from the busy highway in three short benches, each in plain view of passers-by. It was the location that decided it to conventional spring and fall plowings, breaking off and destroying the young feeding roots of his plants as he drove up and down his berry rows. But the sight of rocks, roots and earthworms being thrown up on the surface by his cultivator occasioned some heavy thinking, as did his steadily declining yields.

"By 1936 I got tired of this annual rock crop and decided to cover the rocks instead of dig them up," Stephens said. "The results soon spoke for themselves, and I've been a confirmed mulcher ever since."

The first mulching Rupert tried was to spread two or three inches of marsh hay and straw between his raspberry canes. By the following May the rows were waist high in grass and grain from seed brought in with the mulch. But yield results were spectacular. Money spent to pull weeds was returned with interest by a record berry crop of over ten tons per acre. To add to his satisfaction Stephens noted that his fields had weathered a rather inclement season free of rocks, dust or mud. Convinced that mulching was the answer, he now concen flash fires almost impossible, Stephens reasoned.

"Even these small experiments of mine were looked on with horror by neighbors and friends," he smiled. "They said sawdust would poison the soil."

Leaves of plants grown in soil that has had sawdust mixed with it generally becomes yellowed and mangy-looking. Science has discovered that this doesn't mean the plants have been "poisoned," but are merely starved for vital leaf-growing nitrogen. When any woody plant substance comes into intimate contact with the ground it encourages the growth of soil bacteria to a point where they start to consume reserves of soil nitrogen needed for the growing crop.

DOSES OF NITROGEN

Fully aware of this the Stephens took special care to prevent sawdust from mixing with their soil. They found that even when laid on the surface as a mulch, it stimulated bacteria growth to some extent, and had to be counteracted by liberal doses of nitrogen. Their crops were now bringing from $1,000 to $2,000 an acre. In place of $200 an acre to gather and lay their mulch, costs had been whittled down to from $40 to $75. By 1947 all the crops were under a permanent carpet of sawdust.

No wonder Rupert called sawdust his slave. Apart from the plowing, harrowing and weeding saved, his berries were free of dust and grit. In the wintertime, instead of the usual depressing grey landscape the fields presented a rich patchwork of color.

"Every year I see my contemporaries using bigger and better machines, expending gas and oil to destroy vital fibre and

Rupert Stephens with some of the first of this season's berries.

when the plants started bearing in good quantity that first July. After an unbelievably successful summer, the Stephens were still picking berries when a hard frost suspended operations in early November. Rupert has since developed his own "Goldstream" variety of ever-bearing strawberry, and recently released some cuttings to an Oregon grower so the strain could be propagated there. Goldstreams bear continuously from June 1 to the end of October. The tendency of sawdust culture to retard plant maturity is used to advantage at Berry Paradise with some crops to supply the off-season market.

Mulching is common practice today all over Vancouver Island during dry summer months. Now that sufficient technical information is available on how to handle it," sawdust has become the number one mulch because of its abundance and cheapness. Many growers have been converted to sawdust culture by a visit to Berry Paradise, where a weed is more rare than a strawberry in November.

Britons Don't Resent Queen Getting Yacht

By SYLVIA SHORT

LONDON — "If the Queen wants a yacht, then she can have a yacht," said a London cabbie in reply to this correspondent's query whether he thought Britain was justified in spending $5,040,000 on the recently tries the sea was no barrier, but a highway. This undoubtedly also is the view of the government. While the queen can fly, when making brief overseas trips by herself, or accompanied by her husband, this is impractical when traveling

---

by phases of the moon. In 1940, US pioneer J.I. Rodale started an experimental organic farm and in 1942 he launched *Organic Farming and Gardening* magazine. Rodale is credited with being the first to use the term "organic" with its current meaning of "grown sustainably." Lord Northbourne was the first to use the term "organic farming," in his 1940 book *Look to the Land*. In fact, organic means much more than the absence of pesticides, which is why so many people today buy organic foods.

Today, the United States Department of Agriculture (USDA) defines organic agriculture as a "production system that is managed to respond to site-specific conditions by integrating cultural, biological, and mechanical practices that foster cycling of resources, promote ecological balance and conserve biodiversity." Organic farmers consider the farm an integrated entity, with all parts interconnected. Grandpa Rupert intuitively understood this back in the 1940s, and started to extol natural, sustainable farming and write about his methods.

In the spring of 1951, *BC Farmer* published an article Grandpa Rupert wrote called "Sawdust Is My Slave." It stirred such wide interest that the issue quickly sold out. *BC Farmer* reprinted the article again in a later issue and then it was reprinted in a leading Ukrainian journal in Winnipeg. In 1952, seeking to educate fellow farmers, Grandpa Rupert printed the article as a pamphlet and distributed it himself.

Off To New Goldstream Berry Farm

This month Cowichan lost two residents who have brought much fame to the district.

They are Mr. and Mrs. Rupert Stephens, who have severed their last connection with Mountain Valley Farm, Glenora, and have left for Goldstream, where, as they say, they will "start from scratch", carving a new farm out of virgin woodland.

The couple disposed of the Glenora farm last April to Mr. Raymond Wilkinson and Mr. E. Neville Trueman, recent arrivals from Britain, but remained here to assist the new owners.

With Mr. and Mrs. Stephens it has been a case of "a prophet is not without honour except in his own country". To most residents of Cowichan, Mountain Valley Farm was "just another berry farm".

This was not the case, however, in the rest of Canada and many parts of United States. There the farm was known for the wonderful varieties and crosses of berries which it produced. The farm was also a mecca for professional horticulturists and berry growers, commercial and amateur.

Family Farm

Mountain Valley was a "family farm". It was taken up in 1911 by the late Dr. H. F. D. Stephens, retired surgeon of the Royal Navy, who carved it out of dense woods at the foot of the Koksilah Range. Even today it is walled in on three sides by a thick growth of fir and hemlock.

Following his return from overseas after service in World War I, Mr. Rupert Stephens, son of the original owner, took over the property and found it ideal for the growing of all

Soon the farm became a show place, noted for its high state of cultivation, which had been raised to such a degree that not a weed was to be found on it.

During intervals between growing berries for market and producing plants for other growers, Mr. and Mrs. Stephens began experimenting in cross-breeding and developing new varieties of berries.

Successful New Berries

So succesful were they in this line that their new varieties and crosses attracted the attention and admiring comment of growers and horticultural experts all over Canada and United States, many of whom visited the farm to inspect it and consult with the owners.

One of the odd varieties produced on the farm is a cross between the blackberry and the loganberry. Another was a purple raspberry resulting from a cross between the "black cap" wild raspberry and the domestic yellow raspberry.

An attraction is a ½-acre plantation of cascara trees, which are thriving in domestic surroundings.

To-day 32 varieties of strawberries, 12 varieties of raspberries and 10 varieties of grapes are growing at Mountain Valley, in addition to numerous kinds of berries.

The new Stephens' farm is located near Island Highway a short distance from Goldstream. It is 40 acres in extent and already some berry planting has been done there and bulldozers are at work clearing a part of the ground for immediate cultivation.

During the recent war years, Mr. Stephens took "time out" to serve with the Pacific Coast Militia Rangers, holding a commission as lieutenant under Ranger-Capt. G. E. Wellburn, of the Glenora Detachment. Mr. Stephens credits his wife with playing a great and very active part in the success Mountain Valley Farm has achieved.

Rupert wasn't alone in promoting organic farming. In the early 1950s, filmmaker Christopher Chapman made two documentary films on soil health and founded the first formal organization, the Canadian Organic Soil Association. Other warning voices spoke up against the growing use of toxic chemicals. As early as 1962, Rachel Carson's seminal book *Silent Spring* enlightened a generation to the perils of pesticides and modern farming practices. As these methods took hold, farmers who actively avoided using new and unproven chemicals in food production were called, "odd" or "eccentric," to use a few of the kinder terms.

In the late 1950s, my father, Arran Stephens, dropped out of high school to pursue the artistic Beatnik dream. My mother, meanwhile, was growing up in India, the first person in her large family to attend university. She became a college lecturer in the state of Uttar Pradesh. The two met and married in India in 1969. Their union has shaped the destiny of nearly every venture they have headed, including Nature's Path Foods. Although I tend to refer to my father as the "visionary," my mother, Ratana, has nursed and tethered all of Arran's endeavours, adding her own powerful idealism and nurturing to every shared enterprise.

Before he met my mother, Arran started the Golden Lotus Restaurant in 1967. LifeStream Natural Foods was hatched in early 1971, back when "natural" and "organic" were considered equivalent. LifeStream was the first store of its kind in Canada, with only two other known predecessors in the US: New Age Natural Foods in San Francisco, started by Arran's friend Fred Rohe, and Erewhon in Boston. The back of the LifeStream store in Vancouver housed Ratana's little vegetarian restaurant, the Mother Nature's Inn, which later evolved into Woodlands Natural Vegetarian Restaurant.

In 1971, LifeStream was a founding member of Organic Merchants (OM), the first North American organic trade association, along with Fred Rohe, Michael Potter of Eden Foods, Frank Ford of Arrowhead Mills and a few others. I think they got a big kick out of the OM acronym. As the "back to the land" movement took hold, the International Federation of Organic Agriculture Movements (IFOAM) was founded in 1972. In 1975, Peter McQueen founded Canadian Organic Growers. In the early 1970s, Arran was one of several natural food pioneers who had personal missions to expand the acreage devoted to organic farming by providing delicious, nutritious and organic foods to consumers. Fellow pioneers included Paul and Betty Keene of Walnut Acres, Paul Hawken (Erewhon) and Bill Shurtleff of SoyInfo Center. The logic was simple, then and now: make great products while improving the state of the Earth and of all life. To quote Vandana Shiva, "in nature's economy, the currency is not money, it is life." Organic farming promotes natural processes and biodiversity, and it is a high, noble calling. As early pioneers found success in the marketplace, big multinational companies began co-opting the loosely regulated word "natural," diluting its original meaning, until today it means nearly nothing. "Natural is the most bastardized word in the English language," says Arran.

Conceived in the kitchen of Woodlands Restaurant, Nature's Path was born in 1985. The company's early slogan was "Walking

Rupert with Arran and brother Godfrey.

the path to a better world," and its mission was to "be the change" via supporting sustainable agriculture and minimally processed pure foods. In 1988, Canadian Organic Growers hosted a conference to establish a definition for "organic," out of which emerged the first organic certification programs. In the words of Dag Falck, current president of the Canadian Organic Trade Association and vice president of the Organic Trade Association:

Farmers started the organic movement out of the desire to be able to tell their consumers what organic really was. They needed a system to ensure that those calling their

products organic were indeed growing and handling foods according to some consistent method. Interestingly, it was not consumers who asked for organic standards and certification; it was the farmers themselves who recognized the need for a national organic standard. Maybe it was the consumer within the farmer who saw that faith in organic might be lost without a consistent, quality system with third-party verification to communicate to the customer via grocery store shelves. Even today, the organic industry is one of the only sectors that has volunteers sit on committees where the main objective is to lobby the government for stricter organic standards.

Nature's Path was the first North American cereal company, first Canadian food company and second North American food manufacturer to seek and attain third-party organic certification via a reputable independent certifying body (Oregon Tilth then and Quality Assurance International today). Even the grains of LifeStream's Essene Breads (1971–95) and Nature's Path's first Manna Breads (1985) were organically grown and processed in accordance with Section 26569.11 of the California Health and Safety Code. This was several years before the use of the word "organic" was regulated, which happened in various stages in North America. In the US, the *Organic Foods Production Act of 1990* established standards for production and handling of foods labeled as organic, and in 2002 National Standards were implemented. In Canada, regulations for usage of the word became legally binding and enforceable by law as recently as 2009.

As organics started to gain traction, a new threat to life was launched in the form of foods containing genetically modified organisms (GMOS). In 1996, in response to the alarming developments of the first commercially available GMO crops, Arran said, "there is no wall high enough to keep out GMOs." His well-founded concern was that pollen and seed from GMO crops can easily contaminate both conventional and organic crops via wind, bees, inadvertent or deliberate spills and mixing. Millions of consumers choose organic foods for their families specifically to avoid chemical pesticides, herbicides and GMOS, irradiation and sewage sludge. When national organic standards were first proposed by the USDA in 1997, they permitted irradiation, GMOS and sewage sludge in organic food production. But such public outrage arose that this was reversed in 1998. The USDA standards, covering all foods sold as organic, were officially implemented on October 21, 2002.

Arran has had a hand in designing and shaping the original regulated uses of the word organic, putting the health of the soil and the people first and foremost. A healthy soil teems with microorganisms and life, ensuring a bountiful existence for all, including us humans. A humble lorax, Arran was on the boards of the Organic Trade Association (OTA) and the Canadian Health Food Association (CHFA) when organic standards were enacted. When on the OTA board, Arran warned, "GMOs are going to become the greatest threat to the organics movement that we have ever, or will ever, face." In 2007 he continued his mission by joining the board of the Non-GMO Project.

When eco-prophet Vandana Shiva was receiving an honorary doctorate from the University of Victoria in 2013, she declared, "The growing of food should be an act of love." Amen. In the name of love—for the Earth and all her creatures—Nature's Path continues to strive for quality and innovation in our products. We proudly champion such vital causes including mandatory GMO labeling, farmland conservation, urban gardening, social justice and environmental respect. Our dedication to our core values is why Nature's Path has been recognized over a hundred times for sustainability and leadership, plus numerous packaging and taste awards. At the time of this writing, Nature's Path has been recognized as one of the Ten Best Companies to Work For in Canada. Our story is ready to be told!

NOW ! ! ! the Rush is for . . .
GOLDSTREAM STRAWBERRIES
essence of the MINERAL PACKED BRICK RED, GOLDSTREAM SILT
under the BLUE ROOF of the
GOLDSTREAM BERRY PARADISE
Strawberries from June through October
NECTAR - BOYSEN - LOGAN - CASCADE BERRIES
RASPBERRIES
RED - YELLOW - BLACK - PURPLE
No Spray or Poisons Used
FRESH SWEET CORN
FREE—Shady Picnic Grounds—Sparkling Spring Water
Island Highway at Goldstream, Rupert and Gwen Stephens

Every image in this book (apart from one stock photo) directly relates to Nature's Path: our gardens, our history and our valued team members. Nearly every plant you see in these pages has been lovingly tended by one of our team members or our farmers in the midwest. Even the yogis and athletes you see are our team members. In addition to edibles, my photos of woodlands come from the stunning Morton Arboretum in Illinois.

As mamma bear Ratana says, the goal of this book is "to honour the past, inspire the present and guide the future." In my words: to show our deeply rooted foundations, our team's commitment to people and planet, and to demonstrate our journey in photos and words. Now, in 2015, 30 years after Nature's Path's humble beginnings, I am happy to walk you through the highlights of this wondrous journey along an incredibly lush and fertile path towards a healthier future.

1944–1985

DEEP ROOTS: GOLDSTREAM TO

LIFESTREAM TO WOODLANDS

Baby "Grandpa Rupert" Stephens in the arms of Agnes and Surgeon Commander Dr. Stephens.

Granny Gwen and Grandpa Rupert at Goldstream Berry Paradise.

Granny Gwen loved the feel of the earth in her hands.

Most people get into business to make a livelihood for their families. Some people get into business to change the world for the better. A few actually succeed. Such is the tale of my parents, Arran and Ratana Stephens. The story of Nature's Path begins with my grandfather, Rupert Stephens. Rupert was the son of retired Surgeon Commander Dr. Harold F.D. Stephens of the Royal Navy. At the turn of the century great-grandfather Harold brought his family, including young son Rupert, to Canada from Plymouth, England. He was granted 120 acres in the fertile Cowichan Valley on Vancouver Island for his loyal services to the British Empire. In 1911 he carved out Mountain Valley Farm at the foot of the Koksilah Range.

Both of Harold's sons fought in the Great War and Rupert returned, one of only a handful in his battalion, and took over the family farm. Like many veterans, Rupert healed his battle wounds with the soil. He grew berries and turned the family farm into a "show place," according to a 1940s article in a local newspaper. Rupert's farm was, "noted for its high state of cultivation, which had been raised to such a degree that not a weed

Grandpa Rupert standing with Arran and his brother, Godfrey, at the berry stand, Granny Gwen behind the counter, circa 1955.

Rupert walking through the trees in Glenora at Mountain Valley Farm, 1936.

including "The Bluegreen Hills of Goldstream." This book's title also comes from a song of Rupert's, "This Earth Is Mine," which in the spirit of inclusiveness became *This Earth Is Ours.*

When Arran was about 11 years old, grandpa Rupert took him up into the hills of Goldstream and said, "Arra-boy, this is our church, this is our cathedral." Arran was ingrained with the deepest respect for the earth and learned the principles of farming in tune with nature. The principles behind organic farming are to use practices that most closely imitate natural cycles. The family worked hard, planting corn and berries by hand, weeding, spreading kelp and manure on the beds to enrich the soil and mulching with sawdust to control weeds, retain moisture and, as grandpa Rupert would say, "create an earthworm paradise." One day when out on the farm laying kelp on the beds, Rupert said to Arran, "Arra-boy, always leave the soil better than you found it." Arran and his brother Godfrey (a painter, sculptor and wooden boat builder) remember frequent lineups of upwards of 50 cars to buy their delicious Goldstream berries. The original Goldstream Berry Paradise letterhead featured this apt quote from Isaac [sic] Walton: "Doubtless God could have made a better berry than the strawberry but doubtless, God never did."

was to be found on it." Rupert credited "his wife with playing a great and very active part in the success." His wife was my glamorous grandmother Gwen: a beauty, a gifted artist and a hard worker, who gave birth to my father, Arran, in 1944.

According to a 1951 *Daily Colonist* article, Rupert had been writing songs for 25 years and over 20 were recorded at that time,

Arran often says, "A success is a failure that never gave up." The roots of Nature's Path have grown wide and deep from successes and failures over the years, which taught Arran diverse lessons. My mother, Ratana, always says, "when your father falls down, he just gets back up, dusts himself off and starts again." Arran's first serious occupation was as a visual artist.

Arran, age four.

Arran with Happy the dog, bought from artist Emily Carr. This photo appeared in a local newspaper in 1948

Granny Gwen in her pickup truck.

He left school and home at the age of 15, perhaps in emulation of his charismatic older brother, to pursue art, heart and soul for the next five years, experiencing the highs and lows and infamous excesses of Beat culture, sometimes homeless and penniless on the streets of Venice, San Francisco, Big Sur and Greenwich Village.

Arran's art was first exhibited at the Gas House, the famous Beatnik haunt in Venice, California. There he met eden abhez (the original Nature Boy, who didn't like to capitalize his name), and over the years he honed his craft and exhibited and sold several paintings, including to such celebrities as James Earl Jones.

During Arran's time in New York, along with having his art exhibited at Greenwich Village's Thompson Galleries, he took a job at Paradox, North America's first macrobiotic restaurant. He recalls:

Macrobiotics kind of led to the early flowering of the natural food movement, its commercial beginning. There was Paradox restaurant in NYC, started by my boss and friend Richard Lane; then there was Erewhon in Boston, headquarters for

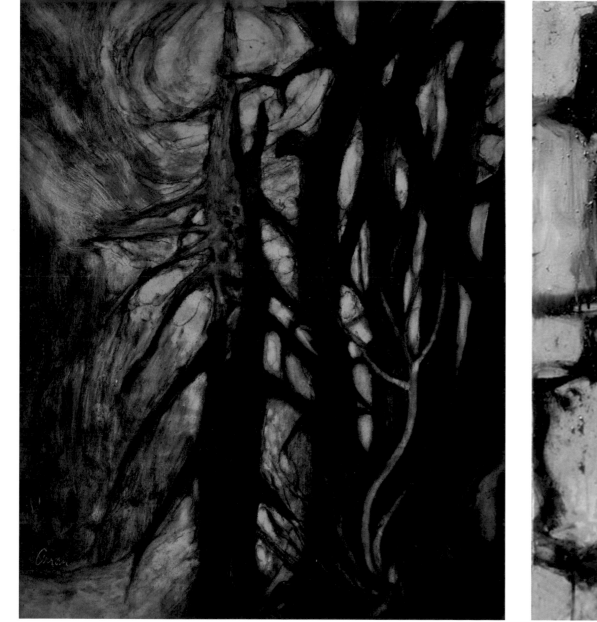

Arran's painting *Cowichan Through the Trees,* 1966, oil on cardboard, 16 x 12 inches.

Self-Portrait, 1962, oil on canvas, 42 x 24 inches.

Arran's painting, which used to hang in the Golden Lotus, *Night Awakening Earth,* 1964, oil on canvas, 4 x 5 feet.

BIRTH ANNOUNCEMENT

Arran Blackburn Stephens

NOVEMBER 12 THROUGH DECEMBER 6, 1963

Oil Paintings
Constructions
Graphics

RECEPTION FOR THE ARTIST: 8 P.M., NOVEMBER 12

Batman Gallery

HOURS: TUESDAY THROUGH SATURDAY FROM 1:30 TO 6
2222 FILLMORE ST., SAN FRANCISCO 15, CALIFORNIA
JOrdan 7-6730

1963 gallery show in San Francisco. Arran had shows in New York and Venice in the early 1960s.

Michio Kushi (the macrobiotic leader after George Ohsawa died); and New Age Natural Foods in San Francisco.

In 1964, in the midst of his darkest moment, Arran emerged from the intoxication and bleakness of the Beat Generation, awakened by a spiritual epiphany that changed his life from beginning to end. (He never did anything by half-measures; it was always all or nothing.) A seeker at heart and an idealist, he

connected with a renowned spiritual teacher by the name of Sant Kirpal Singh.

In 1965 Arran returned to the West Coast and, in 1966, opened the East West Gallery in West Vancouver, exhibiting and selling paintings from both East and West, including his magical realism and semi-mystical paintings in oil on canvas. But in early 1967, he closed his gallery and left everything behind to live in India with his spiritual guide and spend prolonged time in meditation.

Arran meditating under a banyan tree in India, November 1968.

Arran standing outside the Golden Lotus in 1968. Photo coincides with a favourable
article in the *Georgia Straight* by Vancouver foodie and restaurant critic James Barber.

Kirpal Singh told Arran, "Nature is beautiful except when tormented by the hand of man," and "We dig our graves in the kitchen, and more quickly with our teeth." He also subscribed to principles of homeopathy, yoga, Ayurveda and healing through natural methods. Inspired to a higher purpose, Arran felt a calling to bring these life-changing ideas back to Vancouver and give them concrete form. He was heartily encouraged by his beloved mentor, who treated Arran like a son.

THE GOLDEN LOTUS

In November of 1967, with only $7 and a small loan, Arran returned to Vancouver and opened Canada's first vegetarian, all-natural restaurant, the Golden Lotus. In the book *Edible Histories, Cultural Politics: Towards a Canadian Food History*, historian Catherine Carstairs describes the Golden Lotus as a place "where drugs, alcohol and promiscuity were not allowed." Arran says, "I really wasn't a hippie. I could relate to the young idealistic hippies coming through the door, many in a befuddled state, because I had been there a few years earlier." In a comprehensive interview by Professor Carstairs, Arran said:

> The focus was on ethical and spiritual growth as well as following a healthy diet and lifestyle. Many of the young people drawn into this community came from the hippie/drug culture. However, at the Golden Lotus, drugs, alcohol and promiscuity were not allowed. If you worked, you were paid, plus given room and board. Discipline was strict but with strong undertones of love and support.

In 1968, Arran returned to India to meditate and study with his teacher, continuing along a rather ascetic path—until his teacher suggested the wannabe yogi get married! Arran describes the unusual events quite beautifully in his 1999 book, *Journey to the Luminous.* In a 2010 interview, Arran spoke about his arranged marriage, set up by a family friend and Ratana's grandmother. Even though they had never kissed, held hands or even dated, let alone fallen in love, Arran said he felt "loving thoughts" toward his bride-to-be. "We met, got married and fell in love. The physical relationship is not the real basis of a good marriage, it's something much higher and deeper. Our teacher told us on our wedding day, 'you should be as one soul in two bodies, and remain united until the last breath.'"

Little did they know at the time, but Arran and Ratana were to become an indomitable force in food. They fit together like yin and yang, Mom fiery-passionate yet absolutely retiring in public and Dad a calm, inspiring leader, full of ideas and poetry. And speaking of poetry, both my parents published poetry in the 1960s. With their combined energy, intelligence, work ethic, idealism and drive, they would complement each others' roles and create dynamic enterprises in addition to four children and six grandchildren (and counting). Ratana describes some of the early life experiences that prepared her for this path:

My life's journey started in pre-partition India. I was adopted by my grandmother, Bae Ji. She was my greatest influence. At the tender age of 17, she became a widow, and single-handedly brought up three strong-willed, entrepreneurial

Ratana while studying at University in India.

Ratana in 1968, just prior to marriage with Arran.

The newlyweds.

boys. Although illiterate herself, she made sure I finished my university education—the only one in my family. Once, my father, her son, sarcastically questioned Grandma, "Why do you want to send her to college? Is she going to be a judge or a lawyer?" Bae Ji indignantly replied, "Mind your own business. She is my daughter. She will be what she is meant to be." Bae Ji was very strong, entrepreneurial, self-reliant, compassionate and kind.

After settling down in Vancouver, Ratana brought Bae Ji along with several other family members to Canada from India. With her intelligence, strong work ethic and generosity, Ratana is not only a role model for the extended family, she has also been the heart and pillar of all business ventures Arran started after the Golden Lotus.

Kolin Lymworth, who ended up buying the Golden Lotus with Bernard Ross, today owns the iconic Banyen Books in Kitsilano. When I asked him to share some of his experiences at the Golden Lotus, he gave us these words.

In the spring of 1968, I wandered into the Golden Lotus Restaurant, at 4th Avenue and Bayswater in Vancouver. I was a nineteen-year-old hippie/poet/seeker, freshly "hatched" in the psychedelic incubation of the times. So many of us were drawn to the natural, the organic. Having had direct experiences of the numinous ourselves, we were eager to connect the dots around mysticism, natural living and what the sacred meditative traditions of the world had to offer us. We were open, ready to learn.

The Golden Lotus was a popular haven of beauty, with an Indian spiritual vibe—flowered bedspreads draped like exotic tents, shining "golden lotus" candle-holders on every table, Indian ragas on the stereo and the enchanting aromas of frangipani incense and curry. I still recall the series of radiant windows Arran painted above the restaurant with the iconic images of many of the world's spiritual traditions.

The Golden Lotus had one of Canada's first truly vegetarian menus: nutloaf, veggie burgers, seitan steaks, macro plates, great curries presided over by a lovely neighbour, Mrs. Nagra, and so much more. One of my favourite dishes was "Han Shan's Blue Shoes"—every plate entirely unique, a chef's choice from the kitchen that day. You never knew what you were going to get!

Arran was an entrepreneurial wizard, and the Golden Lotus became quite a scene. From 1967 to 1970, the restaurant was a humble and beautiful watershed for organic living and a kind of oasis for spiritual types. Those of us living and working there were young vegetarian meditators "on the Path." Downstairs, lots of hard work (have you ever made halva, seitan, chapatis, by hand?) for a restaurant with about sixty seats. Upstairs, an "ashram" where many of us lived around a meditation room where weekly "satsangs," or spiritual get-togethers with meditation, were held, all in the spirit of Arran's meditation-yoga teacher . . . who also became teacher to many of us.

After Arran and Ratana moved on, the restaurant continued for a year or so as a co-op, finally winding up in the spring of 1970. The restaurant had spawned a natural foods corner, the first in Vancouver, which Arran expanded into

Arran inside the Golden Lotus in 1969 after returning from India.

Ratana in a field near Hope, BC, in 1969.

LifeStream. There was also a book nook, with the few books on vegetarianism, organic living, and meditation and healing that were available at that time. It was from the proceeds I received ($1,500) of what was left of the Lotus at the end that Banyen Books sprouted. Banyen opened in late 1970 just across the street from where the Naam Restaurant is now, on 4th Avenue.

I fondly remember "the Golden Lotus days" as vividly formative. Those beautiful windows Arran painted endured through many later businesses. Some years you could see them, other years not. They finally succumbed to demo and redevelopment in about 2009. The restaurant offered something very few restaurants today can: a friendly magic—a beautiful place to be—with real, good food, made and offered with a lot of love.

Arran and Ratana got married in Delhi in 1969 and Arran's teacher loaned him the money to buy a plane ticket to bring Ratana back to Canada. They lived above the Golden Lotus, sharing one bathroom amongst 16 residents. Things didn't go well:

A few months after returning to Vancouver with my new bride, some of the more left-leaning employees wanted to turn the Lotus into a co-operative—everyone with an equal share and say, even if they did less work. This wasn't for us, and so we sold the restaurant to the co-op for $2,500, and sincerely wished them well.

Arran with baby Shanti, 1970.   Ratana with baby Gurdeep, 1973.

The young couple opened up Jyoti Imports, a short-lived enterprise selling Indian clothes and crafts, a few blocks west of Burrard on 4th Avenue, with an additional location in Gastown.

Although the Golden Lotus didn't last long after Arran and Ratana moved on, fertile seeds had been sown. The "co-op" buyers of the Golden Lotus included Kolin Lymworth and Bernard Ross. With his share of the earnings, Kolin started Banyen Books, Vancouver's (if not Canada's) best and oldest new-age bookstore. A former Golden Lotus cook opened up the Naam Cafe, Vancouver's longest-standing vegetarian restaurant. Bernard Ross used his money to travel to India and came back to Vancouver in 1970 and started working again for Arran. Bernard

now owns and operates a successful software company based in Florida.

An impressive autodidact who had not even finished high school, Arran could also be an innocent maverick. A former college teacher, Ratana wanted her husband to go back to high school, get his diploma and then go on to university. So Arran went to night school, but after reading his essays, an instructor asked him why he was attending grade 10 courses. Right then and there, the instructor provided a direct reference so Arran could proceed directly to university. However, with Ratana being pregnant and both of them working long hours, Arran left university after a couple of semesters. Charged with the energy of the journey ahead, he never looked back.

LIFESTREAM: NOURISHING THE ROOTS OF SOCIETY

After dissolving Jyoti Imports, Arran envisioned a large natural food store selling whole, fresh, vegetarian foods including alternatives to sugar and junk foods. He found an ideal spot in an old building on the corner of 4th Avenue and Burrard to start this new venture, right in the heart of vibrant, colourful Kitsilano, Vancouver's hippy, counter-cultural paradise. Architect Herb Schumann, who had an office up the street, describes meeting Arran for the first time. In 1971, Arran knocked on Herb's door and said, "I'm doing a little reno down the street. Can I just show you?" Arran, then sporting a turban, brought Herb to the papered-up storefront where he had ripped out partitions to

Arran in 1971 or 1972 after acquiring the commercial bakery "The Bread of Life."

Inside LifeStream store, 1971.

the bare studs, exposing the sub-floors, plumbing and electrical. The two men stood on the bare earth between the floor joists, Herb scratching his head. Arran asked him, wide-eyed, "Do you think I need a permit to do this?" Herb was instantly won over by Arran's zeal, charm and innocent naivety. He immediately become a life-long friend, and helped design a safe and sound LifeStream store, trading his work for a couple of large buckets of honey.

The LifeStream Natural Food Store, named by Grandpa Rupert, was the first of its kind. A supermarket-sized store, LifeStream's emphasis was on whole, natural and organic foods. It was not a vitamin shop. The terms "health food" and "natural food" have different histories and connotations. "Health food" is a misnomer, because most of the so-called health food stores carried

precious little in the way of food, and the same is true today. Arran speaks to the philosophy that inspired LifeStream and still, today, drives Nature's Path:

The premise behind the natural food movement can be traced back to Hippocrates' dictum, "Let food be your medicine and medicine be your food." The food you eat is directly transformed into your blood, brain, bones, skin and organs. By supplying quality fuel for this body-temple-vehicle, you'll naturally get more mileage out of it. But, give it poor fuel and it's not going to perform nearly as well, nor travel as far. Eventually, everything wears out. But while you're here, let's make it a quality life. We can do that through quality foods, fresh air, vigorous exercise and other healthy lifestyle choices.

Early 1970s at a natural products tradeshow, after the start of the first organic trade association, Organic Merchants (OM), cofounded by Arran.

Young Shanti in the LifeStream store, around 1974.

LifeStream was a food revolution—the first store and the first brand of its kind in Canada, and the third in North America. As Arran says, when LifeStream opened, "believe it or not, supermarkets weren't even carrying real whole wheat bread!" Most prepared foods were highly refined and contained lard, artificial colours, preservatives and other questionable chemicals. "Whole wheat flour and brown rice were only available in a very few specialty stores," says Arran. "White flour, white rice and white sugar were all pervasive." And then there was LifeStream, with a real working stone mill in the window that ground whole wheat flour! Teachers would bring their students by just to see how real organic flour was made.

We had to educate people that all these "whites" were denatured, unwholesome and fattening . . . The concept of natural was alien to the typical grocery shopper. All of us in LifeStream became evangelists of natural! Some folks dubbed me "hippie capitalist," but I was just a drug-free, long-haired lover of nature and peace who wanted to do something tangible for the world. LifeStream's motto was, "Nourishing the roots of society." The emerging natural and organic revolution was a counterculture reaction, not just to the establishment and an unjust (aren't they all?) war, but to highly processed junk foods.

Ratana was an infant during the bloody Partition of India in 1947, and she had supported her family as an English lecturer at a women's college in India. Having seen her family's hard-earned wealth vanish twice, she is possessed of an uncanny business acumen. Arran says, "she knows how to make a nickel scream!"

Early LifeStream Christmas greeting by LifeStream employee Suzanne Soldan.

In 1971, the concert pianist Victor Yankovitch started Mother Nature's Inn at the back of the LifeStream store. A lovely and incredibly funny man, Victor built a custom coffin (with drawers for his clothes in the bottom) and used it as his bed. He slept in it to continually remind himself that life is "temporary." After about a year, Victor realized his comparative advantage was not in running a restaurant and he went back to playing the piano, beautifully. Ratana bought Mother Nature's Inn from him. After a few months, she boasted that her tiny restaurant was more profitable than the many-times-bigger store out front. Mother Nature's Inn eventually became known as the first "Woodlands." In 1979, Arran and Ratana opened a second LifeStream store at the corner of Broadway and Trafalgar. In 1981, they opened the new Woodlands Restaurant above it.

The exterior east wall of LifeStream and Mother Nature's Inn, mid-1970s, at the corner of Burrard and West 4th Avenue.

THE SPIRIT OF BUSINESS

In 1972, Arran was going through an existential crisis. LifeStream was growing fast and he was feeling overwhelmed with the responsibility. With baby Shanti in tow and me on the way, Arran and Ratana met with their spiritual mentor in Vancouver late in 1972.

I asked my mentor, "The business is expanding so fast, and I'm wondering if we should try to limit its growth?" He looked at me as though I didn't "get" it, and said cryptically, "More opportunities for more people." "I'm feeling the responsibility heavy on my shoulders," I replied. "Then distribute your responsibilities!" he boomed. Later that same year, he said, "To grow a blade of grass is more than a patriot's work."

And, my dad never looked back, sowing seeds both literal and figurative. With renewed zeal and passion, as the store's stone mill churned out organic whole wheat flour, LifeStream expanded into manufacturing and wholesale distribution from a factory and warehouse on 6th Avenue between Oak and Cambie. This revolutionary little company set about making as many healthy products as possible under the LifeStream brand, from the original LifeStream Bliss Balls to Sesame Dreams, organic alfalfa sprouts, organic food energy bars, whole-grain baked goods and the popular sprouted Essene bread. LifeStream quickly expanded again and acquired a bakery in North Vancouver. The first in Western Canada to make a full range of healthy, whole-grain, vegetarian and macrobiotic foods, the company also opened a distribution facility in Ontario.

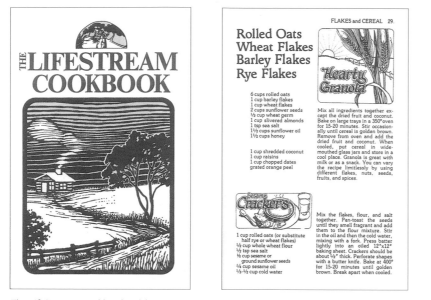

The LifeStream Cookbook sold over 100,000 copies and was reprinted six times.

1970s LifeStream truck.

A founding member of Organic Merchants (OM) trade association in 1971, and in tune and in touch with the other early leaders in the movement, Arran began to distribute LifeStream products into the United States as well as Canada. He also began distributing products from like-minded companies, including from the US. It was exciting for me as a kid to be with my inspiring dad. He was the focal point for all things healthy and alternative. He would draw people in with his passion and zeal, and I met so many unbelievable characters espousing vegan, juice, macrobiotic, mucousless, fruitarian and raw food diets—and this was in the 1970s and '80s, before any of these practices had touched the mainstream. Arran suffered himself (and us kids) through some strange (always vegetarian) diets, including wheat grass juice, which we have never quite forgiven him for! We loved the all-fruit diet but flat-out refused the olive oil cleanses. One of the notable characters we grew up with was Nora Beatrice Lee, who swore off shoes and men and appeared in *Time* magazine as the first woman to drive a big bulldozer. Crazy, fun and cranky, Nora lived with our family for many years and spent her life praising the Lord and giving everything she had to the needy.

Ian Walker, founder of Left Coast Naturals, put it beautifully when he gave a speech in 2013 to present Nature's Path with the OTA award for Organic Industry Leadership. Ian said that, as he was first getting into the natural and organic foods sector, everyone he talked to had one thing in common: at some point, they had all worked with Arran or Ratana Stephens. For example, Member of Parliament Joyce Murray, a Vancouver-based politician who later started up a tree-planting business with her husband Dirk Brinkman, told Ian she'd had her very first job making granola at LifeStream and delivering fresh bread.

Lifestream store, 1970s.

HARD KNOCKS BUSINESS SCHOOL

Aside from his studies in the school of hard knocks, Arran never formally studied business (nor had he gone to art school). However, he is an artist and a voracious reader of books. He initially knew nothing beyond infecting people with his fervour and fire for "healthy planet, healthy people." I remember in grade school when he gleefully showed me how to calculate percentages, something he'd discovered all on his own. In the years since, of course, Arran has had gallery exhibitions of his paintings and has addressed graduating MBA classes at UBC, and spoken at Harvard and other universities. On February 19, 2015, Arran is scheduled to speak at the United Nations on "Food for the Soul."

When first starting his food revolution, however, Arran was lackadaisical about accounting. LifeStream staff would throw all receipts into a cardboard apple box and hire a bookkeeper to "sort it out" at the end of the month. In 1971, realizing this was unsustainable, Arran hired Bernard Ross as LifeStream's controller. Just back from India, Bernard was studying accounting at UBC. "LifeStream was a great laboratory," says Bernie:

> I would learn stuff at accounting school and get to implement it right away. One day I learned in class about computerized inventory control and the next day I said to Arran, "Let's put in inventory control at LifeStream." Arran was always very positive and easy, and he agreed. This system helped us track and forecast sales for over a thousand items

in our inventory and purchase items at the right time. After implementing inventory control, I found that one of our suppliers was stealing from us. We didn't sue him or bad-mouth him. We just stopped dealing with him. Putting in that inventory control prevented us from going bankrupt. We were all so naive and trusting, we assumed everyone was honest.

LifeStream was a wonderful life lesson. I honed my skills, and during my five years as LifeStream's controller, our business expanded from a few thousand in sales to about ten million. It was a special community at LifeStream. We were all spiritual seekers, all young, all idealistic. LifeStream was a foundation for young people to start making something of their lives. To be kind and loving but also hardworking. It went beyond the hippie movement, meaning that there was structure. It was a place to have ambition and integrity all at the same time.

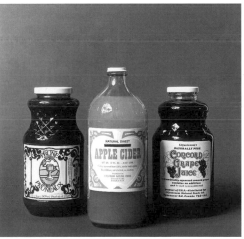

Other early LifeStream products included Bliss Balls, Sesame Dreams, Bird's Nest Cookies, Essene® Bread, Brown Rice Cakes, Eggless Ice Cream, Veggie Burgers, Baby Cereal, yogurts and a full macrobiotic line from seaweed to umeboshi plums.

Apples in Arran and Ratana's garden.

Curiously, this little peace-loving, idealistic natural food enterprise was one of the first companies in Vancouver to use a computer. In the early 1970s, Arran authorized Bernard to buy the first commercial Wang computer to assist in the accounting.

As LifeStream grew, Arran took on two partners. This decision went much against Ratana's advice, and Arran himself would later regret it. In 1981, partnership difficulties led them to sell the company "on a handshake," well below market value, when the company was doing about a million dollars a month in sales.

The sale of LifeStream taught Arran and Ratana two important and painful life lessons. The first was to not take on partners. The second was to not do business on a handshake. Arran's naivety and the culture he had established led him to believe that all other people were like-minded, honest, ambitious and would act with integrity. Arran is an old-fashioned gentleman. Like his father, Rupert, he is as good as his word. Arran realized that it was vital in business to involve professionals who could read and properly interpret the "small print." After hiring a lawyer who wanted to "sue the pants off" a certain person on Arran's behalf, my parents decided, in characteristic fashion, to let go of past wrongs and turn their focus to the future.

Limited by a competition clause, Arran and Ratana decided to expand Woodlands Restaurants to four locations, including 4th and Burrard, West Broadway, Robson Street and Lonsdale in North Vancouver. With another partner, Arran also started up a natural food distribution company called Nationwide Natural

Arnica growing in the woodlands.

Bulk barrels in the LifeStream store, 1970s.

Little Jyoti, Arran and Ratana at their home, which was mortgaged several times over the years to expand the business.

Foods, which purchased the assets of Ardana Enterprises, a distributor of natural cosmetics and herbal products.

Although Nationwide was a success, Arran realized that being a distributor was personally problematic for him because it didn't involve enough creativity or brand ownership. By then LifeStream had been sold to a coffee company, Nabob Foods, which was sold again to Kraft/Phillip Morris. Nationwide provided another lesson: Arran's forte was not in distribution. He wanted to create and build an enduring legacy. My sister Shanti recalls some highlights from growing up in the family business:

Our parents always involved us in whatever venture they started. Our free time was spent supporting the family in every capacity. Sometimes we were human billboards walking up and down Robson Street or Lonsdale Quay advertising the opening of their new retail stores and restaurants. Or spending countless hours manually inputting inventory into rudimentary spreadsheets. While still a schoolgirl, I would work as checkout girl in their retail stores. Helping promote the products at the trade shows was especially fun for us girls. After our work we were allowed to barter our products with other natural cosmetic companies and collect natural

In the early days especially, our family was too busy creating businesses and living in the moment to pose for photos. Here is a rare shot of all four Stephens kids with our dear friend Joan.

lip balms, makeup and natural treats as junk food was strictly banned in the home. Collecting samples from our compliant neighbouring vendors at the fairs was like Halloween in the spring. Our dad was constantly dreaming up new products and new businesses to the point that our mom had to rein him in. He would come home all bedraggled but determined to make it work out. There was always the dream underlying every enterprise—that our family would succeed, that we were all in it together.

Shanti, Gurdeep and Jyoti accompanying Arran on a sales trip in 1982.

ABOVE: Original Woodlands Restaurant sign carved by David Roberts.
LEFT: From the restored prairie at the Morton Arboretum.

WOODLANDS

Woodlands that the winters sadden

The leaves of Spring again shall gladden

So toils an undiscouraged God

And covers the barren fields with sod

And I know nothing that the true

The good, the gentle cannot do.

— ANONYMOUS
(printed on the back of the Woodlands menu)

Jyoti in the wildflowers. LEFT: Ratana next to the Woodlands sign, 1980s.

"When you come across a magic place, listen," read the sign that hung in the entryway of Woodlands. A painting of Arran's hung in the foyer that depicted a man walking, five streams of light emanating from his palm, with a quote by Thoreau, "If a man does not keep pace with his companions, perhaps it is because he hears a different drummer. Let him keep step to the music which he hears, however measured or far away." (Sadly, the painting was stolen.)

In the late 1980s, under amicable circumstances, Arran parted ways with Nationwide, which continues to thrive as a successful distributor of organic and natural foods, including Nature's Path.

Woodlands, under Ratana's management, was flourishing after scaling back to the flagship restaurant on West Broadway. When I was growing up in the 1970s, the only vegetarian foods we could consistently find outside of our home were French fries (if they happened to be cooked in vegetable oil). But Woodlands changed that.

"Woodlands' entry onto the dining scene was as significant as the day that sprouts first appeared in Safeway," wrote John Crawford in the *Vancouver Courier*. "It stands in a niche all alone, having taken vegetarian food into the world of fine dining." He raved about the multicultural menu that included dishes from Japanese, Chinese, Indian, Italian, Mexican and Thai cuisines, and more. "Once these national variations arrive at Woodlands, they are often mixed, adjusted and experimented with until some truly unique recipes are added as 'regulars' to the menu." Vancouver restaurant critic and foodie James Barber reviewed Woodlands in the *Georgia Strait* in 1988 in an article titled, "All the Healthiness, None of the Sludge." He wrote, "Woodlands was spawned by the Golden Lotus, which in its time (when the *Georgia Strait* was not at all straight) was the om center of Western Canada, with meditation the principal ingredient."

I remember my grandmother Gwen coming to Woodlands when I was a tween. She told my parents it would look so much better if all the staff wore white tops and black bottoms. Shortly after my elegant granny's input, the staff got a little sleeker and we all followed a dress code. I recall Dad having to explain to well-meaning but sometimes noisome staff that it was best to wear some kind of deodorant, especially when leaning over to place a plate in front of a seated customer!

By 1988, Ratana championed the opening of the Atrium, which was a finer dining experience than the delicious pay-by-weight full buffet and salad bar. As James Barber wrote, it was "worth it. The Atrium's menu is a multicultural grab-bag—food from all over, subtly catering not only to vegetarians but also to people needing a wheat-free or yeast-free diet" (though, still, the buffet was my favourite). If the Golden Lotus was the om center of Western Canada in the 1960s, Woodlands was a hopping hub in

GATHERING OF THE WAYS DRESSING.

12 fl. oz. oil (1½ cups)
5½ fl. oz. lemon juice
2 fl. oz. honey
1 tbs. basil
1 tbs. rosemary
5 sprigs fresh parsley
2 stalks fresh celery
2 tbsp engivita yeast
1 tbsp. kelp powder
1 tbsp. tamari
4 toes garlic (or less depending on size.)

Blend together. Taste & vary accordingly when increasing quantity.

Mayonnaise

Blend 1¾ cups water with ½ cups oats cook till thick. Mix ¼ cup water with 1½ T arrowroot - mix with oats. Cool
Blend ½ cup lemon juice
¼ cup vinegar
oat mixture
salt
½ tsp each ground dill seed, celery seed, paprika bit of honey.
Blend in oil slowly till thick
Makes 3-4 cups.

Original recipe cards from Woodlands. Our family favourites included Woodlands' famous Spinach Lasagne, Veggie-Butter and Mutter Paneer.

Young Arjan in the family garden. TOP: Arran and Ratana's home garden.

a burgeoning new age, catering to vegetarians, high school and UBC students, environmentalists, the curious, health seekers, and famous singers and actors, including Sidney Poitier, who struck up a friendship with our family.

We kids were taught the lesson of hard work at LifeStream, Woodlands and Nationwide. Providing people with food is a vital skill, involving myriad cognitive and social processes. My siblings and I learned how to engage with folks, provide customer service, keep the tables clear and act cool in the terrifying wake of a hundred hungry customers lined up and out the door. (A hungry man is an angry man!) With her warmth, Ratana made all customers feel intimately coddled. She is the kind of person who gives away her jewelry and shawls to people who come up to her and admire what she's wearing. In addition, my mother has that fundamental ability to keep her eye on costs. She would later bring both of these vital skills to Nature's Path. Our family eagerly looked forward to our annual free Christmas dinner at Woodlands, where all were invited. There would be long line-ups of many homeless and disadvantaged people out the door (and others just looking for company). Staff, friends and strangers would volunteer their time and talents to cook, serve and smile for the 600 or more who showed up. My fondest memories are of singing carols around the upright piano. Our parents have always stressed the importance of selfless service. The Indian word we grew up with is "Seva." We were taught that giving is more rewarding than receiving. This verse by Kirpal Singh encapsulates the spirit beautifully:

The salt of life is selfless service;
The water of life is universal love;
The sweetness of life is loving devotion;
The fragrance of life is generosity;
The pivot of life is meditation;
The goal of life is self-realization.

One of our famous free Christmas meals at Woodlands, open to one and all.

The experiences leading up to the birth of Nature's Path taught my parents that they were a unique combination, each with diverse and important skills. They had learned to inspire people and evolve values-driven organizations from virtually the ground up. Nature's Path was rooted in their failures and successes, naturally fertilized by the premise that one cannot add "foods" saturated with chemicals, additives and preservatives to the body and be healthy in flesh and spirit. They realized that it was important to honour, appreciate and respect each individual—whether customer, teammate or supplier.

1985–1990

TILLING THE SOIL: THE BIRTH OF NATURE'S PATH

When Nature's Path began 30 years ago, Arran Stephens was part of a new generation of health food reformers. Prior to the coming of age of the baby boom generation, health food stores were mostly dowdy places selling a range of herbs and vitamins to a predominantly elderly clientele. This all changed in the 1970s, when growing concern about pesticides and food additives coincided with a thriving back-to-the-land movement and increased interest in vegetarianism, both as a way to save the planet and improve health. Suddenly, a new type of health food business came into being . . . In California, Alice Waters opened Chez Panisse, which stressed organic, locally grown ingredients, while in Ithaca, New York, a cooperative began the long-standing Moosewood restaurant, which is well known for its array of vegetarian cookbooks. In Canada, Arran Stephens was on the leading edge of this movement, first with his vegetarian restaurant in Vancouver, the Golden Lotus, and then with his natural food supermarket, LifeStream. In the 1980s, he started Nature's Path, which would become one of the leading purveyors of organic foods in North America. Through his businesses, Stephens has played a vital role in introducing consumers to organic foods, sustainable agriculture, and the importance of healthy eating.

— HISTORIAN CATHERINE CARSTAIRS, PhD

The photos from these two pages are from our Saskatchewan farms and our Richmond home office garden.

Arran has been called a hippie capitalist, but argues that he never was a hippie to begin with. If anything, he was a bohemian artist and spiritual seeker turned businessman. In his 2002 interview with Catherine Carstairs he explained:

> By nature, I'm an introvert. And as a retailer and restaurateur, I was forced to become more of an extrovert. Sometimes I felt like a carnival hawker, catching a customer's eye and ear, up-selling. It wasn't my nature, but something that had to be done to get the business going, and I was good at it. I/we enjoyed running veg restaurants and two large natural food supermarkets, and did so for many years. But I asked, "Why not do something like Coca-Cola?" Coke took sugared, flavoured, carbonated water, mastered the magic of marketing and created a global brand. I thought, "why can't you take something that's really good and wholesome—that doesn't rot your teeth, cause hyperactivity, obesity and all the health problems associated with the soft-drink industry—and make a success of it? That's exactly what we set out to accomplish, moving from the microcosm of retailing and niche marketing towards the creation of wholesome products, then macro-marketing them, and being amongst the best in the world at it.

Arran has repeatedly said that his goal in business isn't to make money. In a 1985 interview, he said, "I never did this for the money. I believe in this industry and I live my life this way." Years later, he would explain that, "in the early, heady days of

NATURE'S PATH

Arran and Ratana at the first Nature's Path trade show in 1985. All they could afford was half a booth.

Shanti wearing a Manna Bread shirt—prophetic of Shanti and her husband, Markus Schramm, taking over Manna and the bread production 20 years later!

this food revolution, we did it for the love and the idealism of changing the world, to make it a cleaner, safer, saner, healthier place. We did it to support ourselves and families through honest and meaningful work." Brent Flink, who has worked on the team for many years, thought it cool that when Arran told him about getting into business, he was so personally vested in making a change for the better that money was an unintended bonus, icing on the cake. One of Arran's aphorisms: "As the good book says, 'If you're not a prophet, then you're a loss!'"

I grew up with "conscious capitalism" (a term coined by John Mackey with Raj Sisodia, and used extensively by Kip Tindell of the Container Store and other visionary businesses). My father's perennial good nature, gentleness and soft-spoken manner instilled in me the sense that business was an exciting, nurturing proposition, not a cold, hard game of winners and losers, fat cats and cigars. Conscious capitalism has always been one of the tenets of Nature's Path, along with respect for nature and non-violence.

LIKE MANNA FROM HEAVEN

Nature's Path started in the back of Woodlands with Manna Bread® followed by Manna cereals. I remember packaging breads in the back of the restaurant as Dad was eager to leave the restaurant business and become a food manufacturer again.

— SHANTI

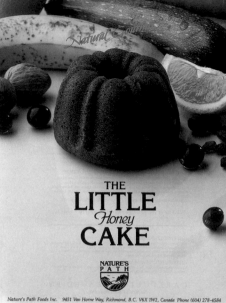

Intriguingly nutritious Manna Bread, the first product launched under Nature's Path in early 1985.

In 1985 the competition clause from the sale of LifeStream was up and Arran founded Nature's Path Foods in the small Woodlands Restaurant bakery. The first Nature's Path product was Manna Bread®, with sprouted organically grown grains, to compete directly with his previous invention, LifeStream's Essene Bread®. Manna was born in Woodlands' little bakery, where talented pastry chef Mina Kulkarni would make the most delectable natural, egg-free pastries and cakes. It was called Manna Bread® because many customers praised it as "manna from heaven."

Manna was an original mini-food revolution in itself, created without oil, flour, salt, sugar or yeast. A moist, cake-like "bread"

was produced by fully germinating whole wheat or rye kernels (which converted the starchy grain into sweet, complex sugars), crushing the sprouted mass, hand-forming loaves and baking them at low temperatures. Like Arran's original Essene Bread®, inspired by a passage in the Dead Sea Scrolls, Manna was a one-ingredient superfood. The Carrot Raisin Manna Bread® had three ingredients. I did many early demos in local supermarkets as a teenager and never tired of watching folks marvel at it.

In early 1985, Arran got a contract with Woodward's Department Stores to stock the new Manna Bread. Nature's Path was soon selling 20,000 loaves a week of sprouted unleavened Manna plus new leavened breads, including Sprouted 9 Grain and Crusty's breads. Manna production soon outgrew Woodlands and Arran set up a commercial bakery in Richmond. Even with the breads taking off, Arran also launched "about a hundred" Nature's Path products, from Veggie-Patties® to a full range of

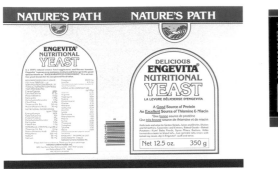

Nature's Path sharing a tradeshow booth with Nationwide in 1986. I used to sell at tradeshows and do store demos. Dad and I were a little team while Shanti and Mom kept Woodlands strong.

macrobiotic offerings, intending Nature's Path to be a complete natural/organic food brand. These other products were not so original and subsided in the wake of Manna Bread and what was to come.

CEREAL ON FIRE

Nature's Path Manna sprouted (pun intended) a dedicated cult following, but was limited by its short shelf life and freezer capacity in the retail sector. The solution came in the late 1980s with Arran's early home-run hit, Nature's Path Sprouted Manna cereals. Former supermarket executive John Anthony, first VP of Sales and Marketing, from 1987 to 1996, says "the cereals were on fire!" With his grocery background and disarmingly charming personality, John helped Nature's Path expand past the independent stores. A handsome, all-round, hockey-playing Canadian, John told me it was an exciting time. He and Arran opened up new avenues beyond the mom-and-pop businesses into wider grocery markets, begging and borrowing shelf facings

from progressive mainstream grocery stores, including Costco, Woodward's and Safeway.

John complemented Arran enormously. An early bird to Arran's night owl, John would often come to work at 6 a.m. to find his president where he left him the day before, having been at work all night. "I think you'd better go home," he would often say to my dad in the mornings. Like many of his generation, John had read Rachel Carson's *Silent Spring* but hadn't understood how to embody the principles. He credits my parents, with their live-and-let-live philosophy, for providing a tangible way to harness the earth-honouring energy and live with deeper meaning.

By 1987 I was a seasoned promoter of all things organic when not in school, playing volleyball or singing. The top photo shows the very first Nature's Path cereals and me holding a bag of Veggie Patties. Below shows me holding a loaf of Fruit and Nut Manna® Bread, with brother Arjan beside me.

Arran has said that, especially in those early years at Nature's Path, there is no position he didn't personally fill. He and John Anthony originally made up a "management" team of two. Of course, my siblings and I would pitch in around our shifts at Woodlands, doing store demos on weekends, filing, making contact lists and being general go-fers. In the early days, my elder sister Shanti worked full time with John to open up untapped opportunities in food service markets:

> As Marketing Coordinator at Nature's Path, I worked under John Anthony—a very affable and voluble boss. I was held to higher standards than the other employees, but wanted to prove my own mettle.

The success of the Manna Flakes prompted Fiber O's, which didn't last—they were too hard!

Following the success of the Manna Breads, Arran invented a product with a longer shelf life. Manna Multigrain Flakes with Oatbran and Raisins was declared Canada's Best New Grocery Product in 1989.

FOOLS RUSH IN . . . AND BUILD FACTORIES

In 1989, the Sprouted Manna® Multigrain Flakes with Oatbran and Raisins won *Canadian Grocer's* Best New Grocery Product. In 1990, it won World's Second Best New Grocery Product at the international monster food show, SIAL (Salon International de l'Agroalimentaire), in Paris. Although ingredient costs were much higher than for non-organic cereals, Arran made sure Nature's Path cereals were sold at comparable prices. This meant taking a much slimmer margin in an already slim-margin business.

Following on the success of the first three major cereal "winners," Millet Rice Oatbran Flakes, Multigrain Oatbran and Multigrain Oatbran Flakes with Raisins, Arran made what John calls "an incredibly bold decision": in the late 1980s, he resolved to open a large state-of-the-art cereal production plant.

Although we baked the breads ourselves, the early Nature's Path cereals were produced by a US co-packer. Arran was not

After the Fiber O's Arran launched Corn Flakes, which would prove a long-lasting staple cereal for decades.

Holding Canada's Best New Grocery Product of the Year in 1989 is Finance Minister Elwood Veitch, who approved the loan to open up Western Canada's first cereal plant. John Anthony and Arran stand on the sides.

confident in the co-packer's integrity, as this was before any third-party organic certification process or standards. Thus began a hunt for land, resources and grants to open up the first certified organic cereal production facility in North America.

Canada's largest bank refused Nature's Path a loan, saying they couldn't see how a small independent cereal company could hope to compete with the big guys. "You'll be crushed!" The government floated a loan for about three-quarters of a million dollars via the Western Economic Diversification Fund. Along with personal savings (including mortgaging our family home), Arran opened Western Canada's and Nature's Path's first state-of-the-art cereal plant, an ambitious 54,000 square feet in

Delta, BC. All the while my mother, who was very profitably running Woodlands Restaurant, resented having her house used as collateral.

That first plant was a dauntless decision that turned out to be brilliant in the long run. But the first few years were brutal. As a teenager, I was repeatedly sat down by my parents and told we were likely going to go bankrupt and would probably lose our home and have to move schools. Disconcerting though this was, I was also told, "money comes and goes." Money is not the goal. As Mahatma Gandhi said, the things that will destroy us are "politics without principle, pleasure without conscience, wealth without work, knowledge without character, business without

Deer jumping the fence on our Saskatchewan farm.

A rare photo of us four kids with our Granny Gwen.

LEFT TO RIGHT: Jyoti, Bae Ji (Ratana's grandmother), Ratana, Gurdeep, Arran, Arjan and Shanti at the ground-breaking ceremony for the Delta plant.

morality, science without humanity and worship without sacrifice." My parents would chime together, "If wealth is lost, nothing is lost. If health is lost, something is lost. But if character is lost, everything is lost." Weary of their ups and downs in business in the late 1980s, they sought advice from one of their Indian mentors, Sant Darshan Singh, which Arran summarizes:

First, keep to quality. Quality should never be sacrificed either for quantity or money. Be honest.

Second, we should expand our business to the extent that we can control it personally. Most of the problems in business come about because we expand beyond our control.

Third, we should be progressive, do our best and make the most of our business, but not be too ambitious. Be cautious: expansion is easy, retreating is difficult.

Darshan Singh's advice proved sound, as Arran reflects 25 years later: "While I have attended many seminars, including at Stanford, and read numerous books on business and personal motivation, this advice captured the quintessence of what is taught in sophisticated and costly seminars. Henceforth, our efforts began bearing consistent fruit."

Initially, however, Delta was a fiasco. The multi-million-dollar stainless equipment was installed in a gleaming, state-of-the-art, purpose-built food-grade facility. For the grand opening, these shiny machines refused to produce any corn flakes—the mainstay of breakfast. Experts flew in and worked around the clock, tweaking knobs and fiddling with dials. But still no flakes! Due to the hoopla of government grant, bank loans and media hype, the grand opening couldn't be postponed. Any further delay would be not only ominous but utterly disastrous.

April 6, 1990, the 94th birth anniversary of Grandpa Rupert was chosen as the big day, and still the machines failed to cooperate and "flake" as they were supposed to. With mere hours to go before the officials and dignitaries arrived, Arran and John panicked and John dashed off to a local Safeway and emptied its shelves of a certain cereal-that-shall-not-be-named. They poured corn flakes along the assembly line and stashed the evidence in a trash container. John laughs, recalling how one guest asked Arran if she could see the line running. Arran replied, "Oh, it's awfully noisy. If we turned it on, nobody would be able to hear themselves talk."

Arran has always gotten the latest gadgets, but he is hopeless at programming DVD players and garage openers, let alone

Whilst the new plant venture was in dire straits, teetering on the brink of collapse, Arran was getting much praise in the mainstream and independent media.

I had never seen Arran so distressed. Even the bagger wasn't working. He said, "Ratana, I don't know what to do." I said, "Arran, just leave it. Forget it all, you can't possibly do more. Just go and meditate."

John and Ratana remember the day the equipment finally started to work. Needing to commune with the divine, Arran drove 20 minutes across the border to the beautiful meditation centre he helped establish in Birch Bay, Washington. At the precise moment Arran began his silent meditation, the equipment finally swung into action, firing out lovely golden crispy flakes. It was a golden (lotus) moment of glory, a full-on chorus of hallelujahs!

At last, Nature's Path revived from the flatline. With the company's heart beating again, however faintly, Arran's vision for Nature's Path would persevere. At this point, we actually had a shot at fulfilling the mandate of leaving the soil better than we found it. With flakes flowing off the line, Nature's Path now had the potential to pay back the bank and the government loans. We wouldn't be on the street, bankrupt, after all!

I wish I could say "the rest is history." But, as Nature's Path started to sing its beautiful song in the cereal aisles, a canary leading consumers out of a coal mine of misappropriated concepts of "natural" and "healthy," threats arose from LifeStream and other big companies. Many trials by fire were yet in store for the Little Organic Cereal Company That Could.

coordinating a plant full of consternated engineers fiddling with finicky machinery. In spite of his optimism, his light started to flicker. He just couldn't do it anymore, with the books already too far into the negative. The company was on the brink of bankruptcy—and still no cereal. Ratana recalls:

March 8, 1985

Nature's Path Foods Inc.
9451 Van Horne Way
Richmond, BC
V6X 1W2

Dear Sir/Madam:

I have recently discovered your Carrot Raisin Manna Bread (M-m-m good!)
and have bought up nearly every loaf that has come into the health food
store on Davie, much to my palate's delight.

My two children are nibbling at it constantly as I have had to resort
to hiding it on occasion so that there will be some left for dinner.
My four year old son calls it "cake" and I don't discourage him.

As my family follows a low fat, high carbohydrate diet without many
sweets, the Manna has become the treat of the day.

The cardiologist for whom I work also looks forward to his hunk of
Manna that has now replaced the store-bought cookies as a snack with
coffee.

Thank you again for this dietary delight.

Sincerely,

Susan

Susan

1990–1999

NOURISHING THE SOIL

Many were incredulous that a little organic cereal company could have the audacity to try and crack the notoriously difficult cereal mass market. Others had tried and failed, having been shut out by the four or five "junk" cereal titans. At a large outdoor food trade show in Los Angeles in 1986, a journalist covering the event was walking past the modest Nature's Path table displaying its first five ready-to-eat cereals, cameraman in tow. Seeing him blithely walking by, Arran stepped out from the booth and asked the journalist if he would like to try a really natural cereal. The interviewer asked, "What makes you think your tiny little cereal brand can possibly compete against the established cereal giants?" and the cameraman thrust the mic into my dad's face. Dad stood tall and shot back, "Well, have you ever heard of David? Have you ever heard of Goliath?" "Good answer!" the journalist said, and that was the sound bite that played all across California on the six o'clock news.

After the Delta plant began producing third-party certified organic cereals, Nature's Path went from the scorching fire back into the sizzling frying pan. And it took time and yeoman effort to

Arran on the cover of *Horizon Air* magazine, 1991.

stabilize and settle back into good rich soil. In 1992, while experiencing significant growing pains in the spanking new cereal plant, the company almost went broke. "We [were] undercapitalised and inexperienced," explains Arran, "but we pulled out of the hole and never looked back." The products were phenomenal, ingredients stellar, quality peerless, vision crystal clear. The problems were financial and operational. As Arran often says, "the Devil, or the Angel, depending on your perspective, is in the details." Shanti recalls:

> We wore many hats, sometimes even working the cereal lines when shorthanded. Marketing and Production were often at odds—I remember cereal being flung by one of the managers in frustration when it was not produced up to standard. Capital was short and there was an underlying worry that we would not be able to pay our bills.

Arran recalls a day when he couldn't make payroll. Despairing, he locked himself in the bathroom until he figured out what to do: approach Ratana! After making him squirm a bit, she loaned him money from the ever-profitable Woodlands Restaurant. She also insisted that Arran take a blanket and a pillow to work because he kept coming home at 3 or 4 in the morning after 18 hours or more at the factory. He almost fell asleep driving home on more than one occasion. Arjan says, "I used to stay up and wait for dad. And he didn't always come home. I fell asleep on the stairs waiting for him many a time." Arjan would have been eight or nine during this difficult period. Interestingly, in later

years brother Arjan himself would also sleep at work; more about that on page 110.

Even after Delta started to produce in earnest, Nature's Path teetered on the brink of the abyss several times. One month after Ratana joined the company full time, the banker stopped by with a briefcase full of bad news. Sitting in front of my parents, he said very solemnly, "Do you know that Nature's Path has broken *every single* bank covenant?" The company needed more time and Ratana told the banker, "We are going to pay back every penny; we will restore your confidence and we will succeed, not because we want to please you, but to prove it to ourselves."

All images on these two pages are from our gardens, grown by Arjan, Arran and the team.

It was that spirit that pushed the floundering company forward through shark-infested waters. When the going got tough in the early 1990s, Arran approached all our suppliers and asked them to bear with the company and give longer terms. "We will pay every invoice off in steady fashion," he promised. My parents always lived up to their word. "Good relations are built on trust and strengthened over the long haul," Arran says. He explains:

> Many manufacturers are always looking for the best price and are not loyal to their suppliers. However, we cherish our long-term relationships with our suppliers of materials and services, including the banks and in paying taxes. We look after them, and they look after us. The supply relationship is as important as the customer bond. It's a virtuous circle based on trusted relationships and shared goals. For many reasons, too many to list, all our suppliers believed in us, our vision, our goal. They trusted us, and rather than seeing our spark extinguished, they preferred to invest in us, with us, not as shareholders, but as valued stakeholders.

A vital loan from our largest supplier for $250,000 kept the sinking boat afloat; as of 2015, this valued supply partner sells more

Shanti, Arran, Ratana and Ken McCormick.

than $20 million of raw materials every year to Nature's Path. Their trust paid off! We honoured one of our honey suppliers at our first-ever supplier awards last year, a great new initiative started by Arjan. This beekeeper I met had tears in his eyes as he discussed the massive bee deaths caused by widespread pesticide use. He said that, unlike some of his other customers, Nature's Path has stood by him and his bees, even during those times when he couldn't supply us with honey.

THE QUEEN'S GAMBIT

We believe in this game; when in business, you go out to succeed at it. Business is a war game, a chess game . . . You don't go out to hurt anybody, you go to benefit your company and all its stakeholders—employees, farmers, suppliers, communities, customers and even the taxman. Make a better product than your competition, and if you can't do that, why even bother?

— ARRAN

During this difficult period in the 1990s, instead of throwing in the towel in this "game of chess," Arran brought out his greatest strength: the Queen. "Ratana was doing an outstanding job profitably managing Woodlands," says Arran. "She had learned the essence of the Japanese proverb, 'Grow a small garden well.' She sacrificed that to help me out at Nature's Path." Ratana joined Nature's Path in 1992 as Chief Operating Officer and was pivotal in turning the troubled operation around. Management of Woodlands was left in the capable hands of Shanti, who recalls:

When Dad first asked mom to help him at Nature's Path they put me in charge of Woodlands at the ripe old age of 20. We were a motley crew: the staff came from all over the world (which was also reflected in delectable international vegetarian gourmet cuisine), and the customers were eccentric, alternative and deeply passionate about our food. The restaurant achieved cult status and our original pay-by-weight system inspired a few copycats. Sometimes our customers

When the Queen is happy, the Land is happy.

would line up around the block for hours waiting to get in. We were ahead of our time in providing food for people following unconventional diets—vegan, raw, gluten-free and organic—years before these became widely available. Mom was busy sustaining whatever Dad created, which left me in charge of the restaurant. Many of our customers were drawn to Mom's charismatic personality, and a few even became family friends. While this role required me to suppress my introverted nature, it freed our parents to pursue their bigger dream.

Shanti got her BA from the University of Western Ontario in 1993 and worked with Woodlands and Nature's Path until 1994, when she married the jolly, German-born Markus Schramm and moved to Chicago. In 1995, Arran and Ratana decided to sell the restaurant to focus 100 percent on growing Nature's Path.

Ratana transitioned from managing Woodlands to focusing her loving care on Nature's Path. "Night and day, side by side, we toiled through overwhelming challenges at the new plant,

In 1992, after over 20 years of living in Canada, Ratana became a Canadian citizen shortly before joining Arran full time at Nature's Path.

Arran plants lots of flowers among the vegetable beds to encourage pollinators and discourage pests.

In the early 1990s, Nature's Path became the second food processor and first cereal company in North America to be third-party certified organic. Here is the back of Arran's business card from the mid-1990s.

resolving crisis after crisis," says Arran. The lesson Ratana had learned from the challenging 1980s Woodlands expansion was to "do few things but do them well." But now she had to learn to think big. "Before, I was selling one meal at a time. Now, I am selling a truckload at a time." Often called upon to share her wisdom, she advises: "focus." Her new aphorism, once she found her groove at Nature's Path, was "why do something small, when you put the same effort into doing something big?"

Reflecting on his 10 years as VP of Sales and Marketing for Nature's Path, John Anthony says, "With all love and respect to your father, we wouldn't have made it without your mother." The three of them formed a management team along with a

controller. Arran was figurehead and driver of the business, but neither he nor John kept tight controls on costs. It was as though Arran rarely had the time to get bogged down in details. An outside-the-box, long-term thinker, he was often miles ahead of the pack, challenging and stimulating creative energy in others. Before Ratana came on board, John would authorize ads and Arran would attend auctions, acquiring new machinery for the plant, liaising with suppliers and purchasing. The queen, however, tethered the two "spendthrifts" to reality, sitting them down and saying, "Every penny spent, I watch."

With piercing focus and evergreen founding principles based on quality first and last, Ratana and Arran learned as they went along and hired stronger, brighter, more skilled people than themselves to work with and delegate to. My mother infused the company with her caring and focus. We who know her well carefully monitor her moods as she is as readable as an open book. Arran installed a plaque in the kitchen, "When the queen is happy, the land is happy." How true it is! When John found out about Ratana's 2013 "Canada's Most Powerful Women: Top 100" award, he quipped, "I'd put her in the top 10."

FIRST MAJOR REBRANDING

The organic industry had started growing from nothing in the 1960s and '70s. By the 1990s, the industry was a far cry from the informal Organic Merchants (OM) group that Arran co-founded in 1971. The torch had now been passed by OM to the Organic Farm Producers Association of North America, which in turn morphed into the Organic Trade Association (OTA) and the Canadian OTA. This organization promoted, educated and protected organic principles and values and served as an effective government liaison in developing national organic standards, forcing all industry members onto a level playing field. (There were a handful of cheaters, but they paid the price.)

The marketplace was beginning to understand organics, as people in increasing numbers wanted to avoid toxic agri-chemicals for their health as well as support sustainable agriculture for the good of the planet. At the time, calling products "organic" was voluntary, with nobody to verify if companies and their suppliers were being honest. Having products and their ingredients certified organic by a third party was going above and beyond what everyone else was doing.

Top two are early logos Arran developed. The other three are legally mandated in the US, Canada and the UK, and accepted worldwide.

Cover crop from Dag's garden. It's fun to note that the seedlings of these plants are on pages 46–47.

Early organic producers were so cutting edge that the rules had yet to be written. Well before any regulatory standards existed, Nature's Path strove for ultimate quality and transparency via third-party organic certification. This allowed us to sell abroad into markets where standards had already been established. Keeping his eye on the prize, Arran developed an organic logo to display on the cereal boxes in the late 1980s (see previous page). In 2002 he affirmed:

> Nature's Path has strictly adhered to the highest organic standards, even before any formalised rules existed—and has been third-party certified organic since 1990—becoming the first Canadian organic food processor to receive this certification, and the second in North America. Many others have recently sought organic certification, now compelled to do so by the USDA Organic Rule if they wish to market organic products anywhere in America.

The 1990s saw Nature's Path's first major rebranding. The first obvious change was the removal of "Manna" from the cereal boxes. Ken McCormick, a former marketing guru for Greenpeace, joined Arran during a time of sparse marketing dollars and huge financial uncertainty to work on messaging and packaging. With heavy input from Arran, Vancouver's leading graphic firm designed the original kelly-green-bordered boxes. Ken McCormick had a unique perspective, with his background in the arts and California Certified Organic Farmers (CCOF), and he put his heart and soul into bringing his deep green ecology message to Nature's Path. In his own words, Ken is committed

Not only did Nature's Path pioneer the use of ancient grains, we created a delicious, nutritious cereal that has supported biodiversity beyond organic.

Millet Rice has been a staple wheat-free cereal for Nature's Path from the very first Millet Rice Manna® Multigrain Oatbran Flakes. Fruit-juice sweetened and nutty-flavoured, it's been one of our best-selling cereals for nearly 30 years.

to "creating a spiritual link between ourselves and the other beings on the planet we share, along with developing the idea of our personal responsibility in establishing a deeper connection to this living Earth." Ken describes the process behind this vital rebranding:

As part of my personal development while working at Greenpeace, I began to realize that the largest negative impact humans have on the planet is not hunting whales or recycling glass bottles, but agriculture.

Around this time, the digital revolution was beginning to turn the graphic production industry upside down, and I was an initial adopter of typesetting and digital production on the Macintosh platform. To help Nature's Path, I sent [Arran]

At that time, sourcing a consistent supply of quality organic ingredients was much more difficult than today, and we were spending lots of money keeping the information on the packages legal and up to date. Arran and I worked closely to come up with a new format I could digitize for easy upgrading of ingredient lists and nutritional information. Also, Arran is a hopeless tinkerer and the digital format allowed him to regularly tweak the images on his boxes and introduce new product ideas.

Arran would design and paint ideas for boxes, including Lonesome Hunny Bear, used on the front of the Honey'd Corn Flakes and Honey'd Raisin Bran (see opposite). We kids especially loved the Einstein he hand-coloured at Ken's studio one night for the later SmartBran® box. Arran could unleash his creativity, working on his strengths of packaging design, innovation and vision, while delegating operations, distribution and finance to my mother and the rest of the team. He was also burning the midnight oil writing his epic biographical spiritual quest, *Journey to the Luminous.*

a few outlines for upgrading the original Manna Flakes boxes to make them more, shall we say, direct-marketing oriented. Like many startup operations, Nature's Path had no advertising budget, but it did have a unique and valuable presence on the local grocery-store shelves, so I grabbed at the opportunity to turn the boxes into stand-alone fundraising programs for the organic food movement, driven by deep ecology principles.

More recently, Arran sketched the original watercolour for the 2012 rebranding of the Nature's Path logo (see page 136). In the fall of 2014, he also made the original oil painting that graces the cover of this book.

With Ratana's vital role established and Peter Tatto's introduction to the team as VP Operations, the company was able to supply the demand that the marketing and sales were rapidly

Arran hand-painted over the "Lonesome Hunny Bear," used here, that Ken began for the front of the box. The bear on the back of the box was 100 percent Ken McCormick.

The first box design for Mesa Sunrise, made with ancient and then-unknown gluten-free cereals like amaranth and quinoa. A delight to sell, it has a large following.

Nature's Path pioneered using ancient grains in breakfast cereals. Kamut Krisp remains a popular flake to this day, available in Eco Pacs.

creating. Peter is now retired but played an important role on the Nature's Path team. Peter recalls:

> It was always my view that the Operations group was to do everything feasible to supply the needs of the Sales Department so they could meet their targets. This approach, along with a strong team ready to support and implement the directions and vision of Arran and Ratana, is what helped the company evolve from a single- to a multiple-facility operation. Being part of this process gave me a sense of personal achievement and contribution. Nature's Path Foods can proudly claim its number-one position in the organic cereal product category.

LIFESTREAM REDUX

When his competition clause expired in 1984, Arran began preparing to compete directly with his former company, LifeStream, as it was felt that the new owners did not treat him fairly. What's more, LifeStream had very deep pockets and vastly outspent Nature's Path in the marketplace. But, as Nature's Path became recognized as an authentic company with a great culture and delicious organic-only products, its popularity increased and its sales eclipsed LifeStream manyfold. Arran recalls:

> LifeStream promptly tried to copy our cereal success, spending millions on TV advertising to launch their line, which was neither organic nor processed in-house. As such,

The LifeStream sea salt packages had a powerful message on the back about Gandhi's non-violent salt-march protests in India.

The original package for SmartBran.

they couldn't compete and thus began their downward spiral. This experience reinforced my confidence in production workers, machinery, bricks and mortar. I was not a fan of the "virtual" company. When making your own products, it's an opportunity to invest them with personal integrity, labour and creativity.

Nature's Path started from nothing and paid its dues. Guess what? In 1995, 14 years after selling LifeStream, I was approached by Kraft, which had bought Nabob. They asked if I would like to buy back LifeStream. We dickered around for a while, and I said, "Under your management LifeStream is losing lots of money and the sales have plummeted. So here's my offer." My offer was dismissed . . . Six months later,

their lawyer called again: "We're prepared to accept your offer." "Well, you've lost this much more market equity since our last meeting, so my offer has just dropped." We ended up picking up the Richmond office building, the brand, factory and all the assets for the value of the real estate.

Two of the best LifeStream cereals were soon converted from the *still*-meaningless "natural" designation to certified organic and rebranded under Nature's Path. Under Arran, LifeStream continued to offer toaster waffles, which we turned fully organic then ended up rebranding to Nature's Path. LifeStream had come to the end of its trajectory in a modern cereal replay of David and Goliath, with Nature's Path reversing LifeStream's losses in less than nine months.

YOU
NEVER
KNOW
WHAT
IDEAS
WILL
COME
OUT OF
A GOOD

BranSTORM

LIFESTREAM

fortified with
17 vitamins & minerals

7.5 g of Fiber - important for busy people whose diet often has more convenience than content

$E = BRAN^2$

One bowlful will convince you that a cereal can taste great and still be good for you

SmartBran
C E R E A L
- *Makes You Think* -

When Arran decided to relaunch SmartBran as a Nature's Path product, he and Ken worked on an image of Einstein. Ken recalls Arran coming to his home to hand-colour and repaint the image used on the original box. It remains a family favourite.

In the 1990s, Nature's Path was given several major awards including BC Exporter of the Year in 1992, an Ethics in Action Award and a lifetime achievement award from the Northwest Natural Foods Industry. More important awards were yet to come. While just pieces of paper and chunks of glass, they do symbolize milestone achievements, especially for such a fledgling company. (For a list of major awards by year, please see page 180.) David Neuman, who succeeded John Anthony as VP of Sales and Marketing and served on the team until 2006, said to me, "It was always written in stone that Nature's Path would be a half-billion-dollar company." When I asked him why, he replied simply, "Because of its foundations." In the 1990s, Nature's Path was still laying foundations for greater successes. And greater challenges.

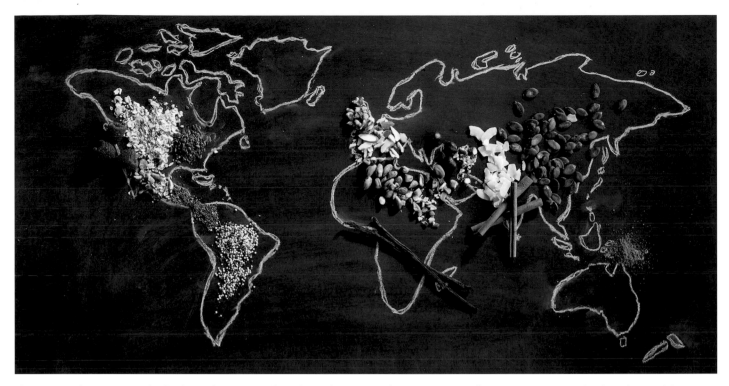

When I started in export, we had sales in the US, Canada and one shipment to the UK. We now sell to 50 countries. We developed a special export packaging in the late 1990s and now have several unique products and designs customized for local language, packaging laws and cultures. Our UK packaging, for example, is quirkier than for other markets, with names such as "Nice and Nobbly Granola" and "Hot & Steamy Oats." And we all love it!

EXPANDING OVERSEAS

I started as Export Sales Manager in late 1997, after Arran had sold a container to the UK. I had moved to Europe with my economist husband, Pascal. After BA and MA studies in biology at the University of Chicago, a co-authored scientific article and a year of PhD studies in Barcelona, I felt my life could have greater impact serving people and planet than studying brain development. After years of relatively mild rebellion, I started to fully appreciate my parents' talents and accomplishments and how I would be all-the-stronger for working with them. I also needed to fulfill my artistic impulses. Singing, writing, promoting organics, living my dreams—I have found much meaning in my family's business.

Residing in Spain, then the UK, I worked to open new export markets in Europe, Australia, New Zealand, Israel and East Asia. In about three years, with virtually zero marketing dollars given to me (because we didn't have them), I grew export from that one container of roughly $20,000 to over $1 million in sales per year. Opening new markets was a fantastic experience, and never felt like "work" because I got to spend time with some of

Mounties, me and dad at the famous monster food show, SIAL, in Paris, 1998.

the greatest, most progressive and thoughtful people and companies around, including gentle, giant-hearted Tim Powell of London's Community Foods.

Our goal is not to sell cereal but to convince humanity of the health, environmental and economic value of the organic revolution. And let us not forget: hundreds of top chefs choose organic produce and grains because of superior flavour. In London I was invited to address executives from the big food companies, including our enormous "competitors." Feeling like a rabbit in front of hyenas, I said that my goal was to convince them to go organic, to support the Earth. I was a little nervous, being a North American 20-something from a little family-run cereal company talking to seasoned MBAs. I showed some graphs and stats and said that we at Nature's Path welcome competition with open arms. My message surprised more than a few, but I was conceived in and born of the idealism of organics.

When sharing the commonsense of the higher goal, I now like to describe Nature's Path using the term *conscious capitalism* (see page 35). It is a great way of encapsulating a relationship approach to business, where everybody wins in the chain: the grower, manufacturer, employees, distributor, retailer and end consumer, as well as the earth, planet, bees and birds—an agricultural paradigm that sustains the health of the soil, air and water.

TAKING AN EARLY STAND AGAINST GMOs

Past experience with powerful new technologies like nuclear power, DDT and CFCs teaches us that our ignorance is great and there are always unintended consequences. Genetic engineering represents manipulation with the very blueprint of life in ways that never occur in nature. In releasing GMOs into open fields or waters or into the food stream, we are performing an experiment, and I believe we should be far more cautious and humble.

— DAVID SUZUKI

In the 1990s, Arran was one of few North American leaders in any industry rightly questioning the place of GMOs in Nature. He has lobbied the government to implement the precautionary principle as have countless citizens of 64 other nations. Arran was a founding board member of the Non-GMO Project and has been standing up against this unsafe and unproven technology since 1996. John Fagan is a molecular scientist whose expertise in GMOs is recognized worldwide. John recalls the first time he worked with Arran:

My first encounter with Nature's Path and with Arran was when the Canadian Health Food Association invited me to testify at a meeting with Cabinet Members and Members of Parliament at the Parliament in Ottawa. Arran played a key role in organizing the meetings, and he also assured we were all well fueled and energized on the morning of the meeting by making sure we had plenty of Nature's Path cereals for breakfast. It was the perfect start of a day of tough

David Suzuki, environmental hero.

Note the non-GMO claims on the front left of both cereal boxes. The company was bullied into removing these.

discussions, where Arran spoke passionately and lucidly about his concerns both as a citizen and as the founder of one of North America's pioneering organic food companies.

He shared his vision with love and compassion at the same time as he was uncompromising in making it clear that GMOS were an affront to the food system. He also affirmed that our food system should be much more than just free from GMOS. That day was my introduction to the standards that have underpinned Nature's Path from the first,

delivered by the visionary that created them, with inspiration from his father.

In December 1997, the USDA published their original organic rules document with egregious exceptions. "The public and the organic community responded to it with outrage," says Ken McCormick, "particularly since the USDA recommended *that GMOS be included* in organic production." Ken recounts the company's bold move to put the "No GMOS" label on packages:

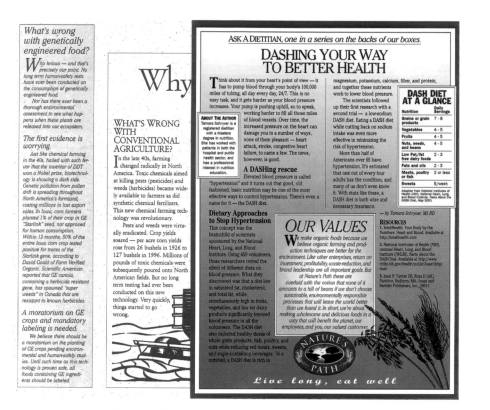

Arran and Ken got subversive and moved the non-GMO message onto the *inside* of the box! Here is a box I cut open so you can see the back outside and two panels from the inside.

Between January and April 1998, the GMO issue was extensively discussed among all members of the organic industry, and that is when the No-GMOs package labeling issue came to the forefront. Nature's Path took a leadership position in the organic trade by being among the first to put the "No GMOs" statement on their boxes. My best guess is that those boxes would have arrived on the grocery store shelves in late 1998. Reaction from [a large supermarket chain]

would most likely have come in late 1998 or early 1999, with Nature's Path responding to being forced to take the statement off its boxes by taking out public ads against GMOs in the later part of 1999.

Arran continues the story:

Before the Non-GMO Project verification began in the late 1990s–early 2000s, Nature's Path was being intimidated by a national grocery association to remove all references to GMOs from our boxes or face a boycott from members.

Pollinators come in all shapes and sizes. Here is one on a buckwheat plant.

This organization represented over 70 percent of grocers in Canada, and it would have meant layoffs and financial disruption for our company. So, what Ken and I came up with was removing the GMO references from the outside of the boxes, only to move them to six big billboards INSIDE of every carton! It was subversive, and our customers loved it! Eventually the Grocery Council of Canada backed off, as did our largest Canadian customer. Within a few years, these same grocery stores accepted the non-GMO message.

For more information and my understanding of how GMOs negatively impact organic farming and nature, please see the appendix. I'll give the last word here to Ken Roseboro, editor and publisher of *The Organic & Non-GMO Report:*

Nature's Path offers the greatest example of a business that is committed to producing nutritious and wholesome organic and non-GMO food. Nature's Path is a company that "walks the talk" with its unwavering commitment to organic farming and food. Nature's Path has also been THE leading organic company in raising awareness of the threats posed by genetically engineered foods, fighting to keep them out of the food supply and for consumers' right to know if foods contain GMOs and in working to ensure consumers have verified non-GMO choices. If there were more businesses like Nature's Path, the world would be a much better place.

Most recent "look" of Eco Pacs® (as of 2012).

The second major Eco Pac® phase.

OUTSIDE OF THE BOX

One of John Anthony's many career highlights was the launch of the economical and ecological Eco Pac®, a large, recyclable cereal package that eliminates the outer carton and reduces package size. Originally, Eco Pacs were offered in pillow packs only to the natural food trade. The higher-volume Eco Pacs resulted not only in cost savings up and down the line, they also gave an edge to the smaller independent stores and co-ops.

The first Eco Pacs were hand-stickered right off the assembly line. Gradually, these were upgraded to a two-colour, then full-colour printed, stand-up bag. Bringing the flakes out of the box like this was a first. Saving on boxes was a double win, saving money and resources. Eco Pacs ended up being copied by most of the industry, but it was Nature's Path that ultimately triumphed in the marketplace.

ENVIROKIDZ®

In the 1990s, we kept hearing, "I love your cereals, but I can't get my kids off their sugary, artificially coloured, herbicide- and pesticide-laden cereal." Surprisingly, I heard this both from movers and shakers in the organic and natural food industry and from mainstream consumers. For the team, coming up with an organic option to a generic "kid's" cereal didn't seem particularly interesting. What was the higher purpose? I, however, had concrete plans to enter motherhood at this time, so I was enthused when Nature's Path started developing the EnviroKidz® line in the late 1990s. The boxes from the get-go were captivating, with realistic depictions of endangered species, such as Jimmy Gorilla (whose teeth Dad insisted on "fanging down" so as not to give little kids nightmares!).

Unsustainable agriculture is perhaps a larger threat to our planet and health than poaching or deforestation. However, deforestation and unsustainable agriculture are inextricably linked. Moreover, most of us feel connected to the animals our species is relentlessly wiping out. EnviroKidz is a win-win cereal on so many levels. It directly supports organic agriculture, uses recycled packaging (relatively uncommon when we started) and is gluten-free and lower in sugar than conventional brands. In addition, we donate one percent of the sales from every box to help threatened species and environments.

If Nature's Path were a public company, the shareholders would probably rather receive that 1 percent as a dividend. Being a family-owned independent company allows us to stand up for the causes we are passionate about. In fact, we've been supporting many charitable partners since the launch of EnviroKidz, working with our partners to tell their stories on the outside and inside of the boxes. As of 2015, we have a dozen partners and projects, including:

- **Amazon Conservation Team**—Teaching indigenous children about their traditional culture and local ecosystem to foster the next generation of rainforest stewards.

- **Australian Koala Foundation**—Protecting the koala and its habitat.

- **Defenders of Wildlife**—Wildlife and habitat conservation and the safeguarding of biodiversity throughout North America.

- **Dian Fossey Gorilla Fund International**—Conserving and protecting gorillas and their habitats in Africa.

- **Fauna & Flora International**—Preserving biodiversity in the developing world.

- **Jane Goodall Institute**—Supporting projects and young leaders across the Congo Basin.

- **Lemur Conservation Foundation**—Preserving primates of Madagascar through conservation, lemur propagation, education, art and research.

- **See Turtles**—Protecting endangered turtles throughout Latin America and the world by supporting community-based conservation efforts.

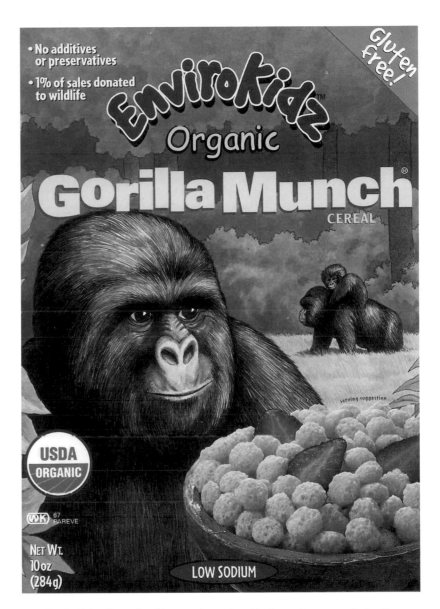

2013 EnviroKidz rebranding. To spend an enjoyable time, please google "rustle my jimmies" and learn about the hilarious movement of early gorilla fans.

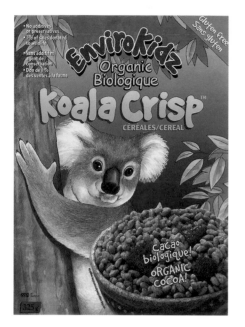

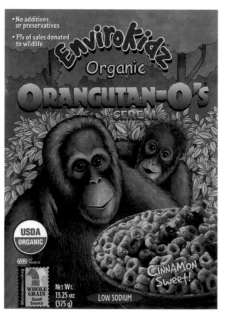

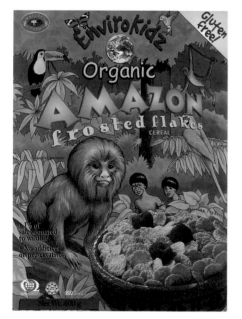

Early EnviroKidz® packages.

The new look of EnviroKidz® launched in 2011–12.

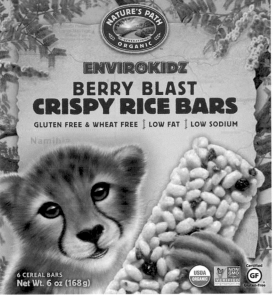

Early packaging.

New bar packaging.

When I was living in London, I was thrilled to record some of Grandpa Rupert's songs as a giveaway to EnviroKidz purchasers who had collected a certain number of boxtops. Over $2.3 million dollars have gone to support various EnviroKidz environmental charities over the years. A father shared with us that his daughter is now in college studying primatology because of a message on the Gorilla Munch box. In the words of a Nature's Path slogan, "Wake up, go to work, change the world!"

In 2013, EnviroKidz went through a rebranding. While this was a good move for our brand identity, the switch to a baby gorilla "rustled the jimmies" of a few fans. We were surprised to learn that the original gorilla had a cult following. Here's hoping our early gorilla fans will be pleased to see him honoured in these pages.

Jyoti holding new Nature's Path Flax Plus®.

FLAX REVIVAL

After reacquiring LifeStream in 1995, Arran and the team decided to launch some new LifeStream cereals. Around this time, Arran attended a nutraceutical conference sponsored by the University of Guelph, where an agriculture professor spoke extensively about the health benefits of flax seed. In ancient times, flax seed (aka linseed) was recognized for its superior nutrition; both Charlemagne and Caesar ordered their soldiers to consume a handful of flax seeds daily. In North America, flax had been used primarily for non-human consumption, such as linseed oil for paint. In the UK, most consumers I met recognized

First LifeStream cereals Arran and team launched after the LifeStream repurchase.

it as the oil they used for their cricket bats! Flax seed contains high levels of omega-3 and -6 fatty acids. Along with hemp, flax oil is prized by vegetarians seeking non-animal sources of these essential amino acids. Interestingly, the beautiful blue flax flower (see photo opposite) grows anew each day and falls to the ground in the evening. A farmer can calculate the yield in bushels based on how many days the plant continues to flower.

Arran returned home from the conference inspired, and immediately began developing a great-tasting new cereal called Flax Plus®. Nature's Path was already using flax in its Mesa Sunrise, developed in the early 1990s. Flax Plus® was introduced as a new cereal flake in 1996–97. Soon a best-seller, Flax Plus® remains popular to this day. Other Nature's Path products containing flax are Optimum®, waffles, hot oatmeals, granolas and granola bars.

Beautiful blue flax flowers fall off each night and regrow the next morning.

79

Arran with Dieter and Barbara Schugt, mentors and friends.

FRIENDS IN BLAINE

By the end of the 1990s, Nature's Path had grown larger and faster than anyone's wildest expectations. Arran wanted to provide new forms of cereals—not just flakes, O's and mueslis, but also puffs and blends, granolas and flavoured oatmeals. The Delta plant was churning out flakes at maximum capacity, and we desperately needed to expand. My parents made a critical decision to exit the private label business and focus on marketing the Nature's Path brand exclusively. Ratana says, "In the absence of a brand, price becomes your brand." Besides, Nature's Path could barely keep up with the demand for its own brand. The search for a second plant was set in motion.

LEFT TO RIGHT: Blaine mayor John Hobberlin, Senator Georgia Gardner, sign-carver and friend David Roberts, Arran and Ratana, 1997.

Family friend, mentor and future mayor of Blaine, Washington, Dieter Schugt suggested that Nature's Path cross the border and set up a production facility in Washington State. Blaine welcomed Nature's Path as a valued addition to the town's economy and a corporate leader they could all feel good about. What town doesn't want a healthy food operation committed to people and planet? They even named our street "Nature's Path Way."

LEFT TO RIGHT: Gurdeep, Arjan, Arran, Jyoti, Shanti, Chaiji (Ratana's mother) and Ratana, 1997.

State-of-the-art cereal manufacturing plant under construction in Blaine in 1998.

Neighbours often compliment us on the nice aroma of toasted cereal emanating from the cereal plant!

A brand-new, state-of-the-art facility was built. This time, when Ratana refused to put up the family home as collateral, the banker capitulated to her demand; after all, the company had long ago emerged from debt. The grand opening of the 60,000-square-foot facility was a "family affair," as covered in *The Northern Light* in August 1999. My uncle Godfrey carved a large red cedar abstract sculpture, *Sea Scroll*, for the foyer of the new

building, and my sister Jyoti and I sang a couple of Grandpa Rupert's songs, including "This Earth Is Ours." Eric Andrew, Senior Partner at PriceWaterhouseCoopers, was moved to tears by the occasion. Eric offers his observations on Arran, Ratana and his years of association with Nature's Path:

I started working with Arran and Ratana and their team in 1990, when Nature's Path was a small, struggling startup, and I have been privileged to watch the company grow over the past 25 years into a vibrant, successful, visionary

LEFT TO RIGHT: Shanti, Ratana, Arran, Jyoti, Gurdeep and Arjan in August 1999 at the Blaine plant grand opening.

organization. Arran and Ratana have a unique combination of skills that has fuelled Nature's Path's success in a significant way. It isn't often that you see a business developed in equal partnership by a couple with such complementary skills: Arran with his clear vision of how to make the earth a better place and develop the organic food industry decades before others, his hands-on approach to developing innovative new products and his courage to tackle the next challenging and sometimes bold but risky step. Ratana fiscally prudent and ready with a backup plan, never willing to bet the farm. She is always hands-on in the details of the operations and people, always encouraging people to stretch and grow, but there to catch them if they fall—everyone's surrogate Mom.

Blaine mayor John Hobberlin helped cut the ribbon at the grand opening of the factory, and hearty congratulations poured in, including from Washington Governor Gary Locke. The *Bellingham Herald* reported:

Once associated with sprout-eating hippies, the natural and organic foods niche has become popular enough to expand from natural food stores to mainstream supermarkets in Whatcom County and across the nation . . . The Blaine factory is a microcosm of the booming demand, with industry experts projecting that sales of organic cereals will increase 54 percent over the next 5 years.

Dear Nature's Path people,

My name is Brendan, I am 8 years old and I just wanted to tell you how much I love your Oaty Bites cereal. To me, it tastes like creamy vanilla cereal. When me and my mom go shopping I always make sure to tell her to buy me a box of Oaty Bites for breakfast. I just love Oaty Bites! I also like the Nature's Path Gorilla Munch and we use your Crispy Rice to make crispy treats!!! Before we discovered Oaty Bites we had Blueberry Cinnamon Flax and it was yummy. Then we discovered Heritage Bites! Then, my mom went shopping one day and bought some Oaty Bites for my little brother, I tried some and they were delicious!!!!!!!!!!!!!!!!!!!!!!!!!!!!!!!!!!!! Ever since then, I love Oaty Bites.

Sincerely,

Brendan

Brendan P.

P.S I Typed this myself!

83

2000–2010   **SOWING THE SEEDS: INTO THE MAINSTREAM**

Ratana and Arran holding their award from the Canadian Health Food Association, 2003.

Arran holding Entrepreneur of the Year award. Nature's Path was also given a National Citation for Product Development and Marketing Excellence.

Back in the seventies I predicted that the day would come when organic foods would become mainstream. This was something too good and commonsensical to be contained within a tiny niche. It needed to be liberated and integrated into the main. Our company had to become strong, with a solid financial base, so as not to be wiped out by real competition when it inevitably came. I sensed the need to gain control of our production, and a race began, to build, brick by brick, a solid foundation that could withstand the storms.

— ARRAN

When my parents started LifeStream, there was no organic industry, just a bunch of wild-eyed, passionate food fanatics like the folks who formed the short-lived OM (Organic Merchants) in 1971. By the 2000s, after continuous efforts and education, passion and perseverance, organics started to really pierce the mainstream, especially after the Organic Standards were accepted and made law. In contrast, the term "natural," which remains relatively meaningless, has never been adequately regulated. In fact, some consumer groups have successfully sued companies, forcing them to remove the offending "natural"

Nature's bounty from our Richmond home office garden.

claims because it is false advertising to label foods as "natural" when they contain GMOs, pesticides, herbicides and fungicides. To recap developments: in 1990, the US Organic Foods Production Act proposed standards for production and handling of foods labeled as organic, but with an unfortunate twist: the government would allow GMOs, irradiation and sewage sludge into organics, rendering the Act meaningless. In 1997, when these standards were submitted, there was outrage from the public and industry stakeholders. By 1998, the protests had their effect, and irradiation, GMOs and sewage sludge were disallowed in all organic farming and processing. In October 2002, all foods sold as organic were covered by USDA standards. In 2009,

View of Arran and Ratana's home garden.

the regulations in Canada regarding usage of the word organic became binding.

With these new standards, global consumer goods companies wanted to get into the action. On one hand, this is the "organics going mainstream" that people like Arran always dreamed of. But, were the multinationals really dedicated to the ideals of organic land stewardship or did they just want a piece of the pie—or the whole pie? In 2015, only a very small handful of the original iconic brands still hold their ground, refusing to sell out. The others have fallen under the huge umbrellas of the big multinational grocery brands, or have perished.

Many of the world's largest multinational consumer packaged goods companies behave in perplexing ways. In North America, almost without exception, they are members of the Grocery Manufacturers Association (GMA), which is fighting tooth and nail to prevent labeling of GMOs. Ironically, these same companies that label GMOs in dozens of other countries or reformulate their products to not contain GMOs hide behind the GMA in North America to oppose the basic right for citizens to know if their food contains GMOs. These same multinationals create an angry disconnect with informed consumers when they purchase an organic brand and switch a certified organic cereal or yogurt to a "natural" label, with no decrease in price (cheaper ingredients, higher profit). As Arran explained in 2002:

Worshiping organic farmers on the backs of our boxes.

Arran planting seeds in his home garden.

LEFT TO RIGHT: Arjan, Jyoti, Ratana and Arran.

When an independent is sold to a large multi-billion-dollar conglomerate, often the soul is gutted. There's a culture crisis. And the acquirer, of course, just gets bigger and bigger. Although competitors have been largely gobbled up to become three or four gigantic corporations, ironically, this has sometimes been to the benefit of the remaining independent operators, because the acquirers often lose the original focus. As one of those independents, Nature's Path must maintain a laser-sharp focus . . . While remaining true to our original vision and grassroots, we simply cannot restrict the benefit of health and sustainability to only a fringe.

We're in the crosshairs of some big competitors. Why? Because their core business is flat and they've seen the

growth potential in organics. Their raison d'être, however, is quite different from that of Nature's Path and our founding vision. One is born of opportunism and the other is born of vision, purpose and commitment. If they don't realize big gains fast, they'll be out in a flash, but we'll still be there.

Fortunately, thanks to the stringent regulations for the designation of organic, if a brand has the USDA or Canada Organic logo, the consumer can trust the product. To bear this logo in either country, a product must, by law, contain a minimum of 95 percent organic content (salt, for example, is a minor ingredient and cannot be grown organically).

Blueberry blossoms in my home garden.

OPTIMALLY OPTIMUM

Within a year of Blaine's grand opening, we had to double that plant's capacity from 60,000 to 120,000 square feet and grow the team to over 200 valued members. The "Little Organic Cereal Company That Could" was picking up speed after the rough "I think I can" early hills. The Optimum range of cereals helped bring Nature's Path to a new (albeit temporary) plateau.

David Neuman, then VP of Sales, recalls sending Arran an email after being struck by inspiration while training for a marathon. Having just read *8 Weeks to Optimum Health* by Dr. Andrew Weil, David suggested a cereal that combined protein, complex carbs, blueberries and flax. It was going to be a complicated and costly product to manufacture, requiring us to make and blend

Up until Blaine's opening, we made mostly flakes. Now an explosion of products occurred: puffs, granolas, bars, shapes, shredded cereals, hot oatmeals, toaster pastries and ingredients.

Blueberries in Arran and Ratana's garden.

Jyoti on the back of the Optimum® Zen box.

five different cereals, including flakes, bran threads and puffs. Despite the challenge, Optimum® Power Cereal turned out to be a winner and a turning point. Although Flax Plus® was an earlier successful functional food cereal, Optimum® appealed not just to our core consumer but also to the wider fitness consumer base looking for all that Optimum® offered in nutrition, taste and uniqueness.

I have been with Nature's Path for 17 years and the time has flown by. I was always intrigued by the supplier side. Prior to Whole Foods I worked with Coca Cola and really enjoyed the selling and relationship building that came with that. I first met Arran Stephens at Expo East all those years ago and after spending about an hour with him and learning more about the company, the products and the future plans, I knew then it was the place I wanted to be. I was promoted to National Sales Manager a few years later, then VP of Sales. We have grown the Nature's Path brand in many categories from a top 10 brand to the #1 position in the organic food industry, selling in the natural, grocery, club and mass channels today in 50 countries. This journey has been so rewarding. I really enjoy the excitement of making organics available to the world!

— CHIP GOBLE, VP Sales

One of my favourite promotional T-shirts reads, "Take 1 bowl, two hours before winning."

95

Jyoti wearing my jeans and organic cotton shirt in Brazil. Jyoti was the original inspiration for my blog's "Style-Diet Shot," which celebrates organic, ethically made local and repurposed clothing.

SUSTAINABILITY

Sustainability is the key to our survival as a people, a society and a company. At Nature's Path, we envision ourselves as leaders respectfully moving towards a healthier, more secure world. We want to help leave the planet better than we found it.

— JYOTI in *Waking up the West Coast*

My younger sister, Jyoti, has been a longstanding champion of social and environmental justice. After getting her BA in sociology from the University of Victoria, and occasionally moonlighting as a jazz singer, she saw a little bit of the world and found herself back at Nature's Path, this time in the marketing department working under Rob Wardle in the early 2000s. Following a trip to the 2004 Bioneers Conference in California, Jyoti came back inspired with a vision for what we could do to make our company more sustainable. She shared her idea with Arran and Ratana, who gave her the opportunity to put her idealism into action through formalizing our sustainability mandate.

Jyoti took on the role of Sustainability Manager and in 2007 was awarded an MBA from the Bainbridge Graduate Institute at Pinchot. This "green" MBA program in Washington State unites students dedicated to applying their skills towards ideals of conscious capitalism and environmental sustainability.

Though a self-described introvert, Jyoti's calm, common sense and empathetic personality make her a natural with people. Her vision, leadership ability and dedication to strengthening the company's sustainability initiatives have attracted like-minded evergreen idealists into the Nature's Path fold. Working alongside fellow BGI alum Jason Boyce, Jyoti and her team have helped redesign, resize and reduce our recycled boxes, rewarding us with 10 percent material savings plus improved shipping efficiencies and shelf presence. The team has also spearheaded on-site initiatives through subsidies for green transit. One of our campaigns, "Wake up, go to work, save the world," expresses

Jason Boyce, Sustainability Manager.

the ethos of our amazing team members. Jason speaks for many when he describes the inspiration he finds in his work with Nature's Path:

> I worked for years in the charitable world helping educate, advocate and innovate towards a more sustainable planet. While I was doing that, I found myself increasingly inspired by businesses I worked with that would put into action the things I advocated for. I would strive to educate or change opinions, while a business owner would just decide to change their buying practices—and overnight, what was once impossible became probable.
>
> — JASON BOYCE, Sustainability Manager

Thanks in large part to the efforts of Jyoti and the team, Nature's Path has been recognized multiple times as one of British Columbia and Canada's greenest employers. In 2007, Jyoti won a competition fellowship with the Royal Society of Arts (UK) and Gold in the Burns Bog Conservation Society Celebrating Women and the Spirit of the Cranes. She was also the runner-up

footprint, areas which were later distilled into 5 main goals (see page 161). In 2011, Nature's Path's Sustainability Manager, Jason Boyce, became a board member and the company continues to support the SFTA to this day.

To share our goals of sustainability with the world, Nature's Path launched an engaging educational campaign in 2010. Maria Emmer-Aanes, Nature's Path's first Communications Director, announced at the time:

> We want this campaign to motivate people to learn more about the path to sustainability without any of the green guilt. We've tried to make the campaign fun, quirky and a bit tongue-in-cheek to let people know that sustainability is a journey and that we all make mistakes along the way, but that the point is to get started.

My favourite part of the sustainability campaign was an expanded aphorism, "Steps to Sustainability":

> Step 1. Mow your own grass.
>
> Step 2. Use a hand-powered lawn cutter.
>
> Step 3. Let your grass grow.
>
> Step 4. Obtain a goat.

In 2014 Jason worked with fellow SFTA members, including Annie's HomeGrown, Sunopta, Organic Valley, Organically Grown Company, Strauss Family Creamery and Turtle Mountain,

naturespath.com/getonthepath

to launch the first organic food industry code of conduct for supply chains. This voluntary code is a way to enshrine basic labour, environmental and social sustainability standards in the organic industry. According to a 2010 article by Jane Hoback in *Natural Foods Merchandiser:*

> The company is now proving that sustainability doesn't have to be tedious and expensive . . . The results of Nature's Path's

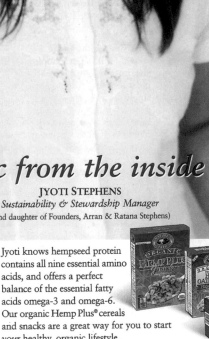

sustainability efforts read like an environmental statistician's dream. The company says its new, smaller Eco Pacs . . . save 825,540 gallons of wastewater, 437 tons of paperboard, 7,464 million BTUs of energy and 1.4 million pounds of carbon dioxide. Nature's Path's new, smaller granola boxes conserve more than 34 tons of cardboard and 65 tons of paperboard, and its reduced-size granola-bar boxes save 472,000 gallons of water and 50 tons of waste.

Jyoti and Jason expound on some of the company's people and planet nurturing over the past decade or so:

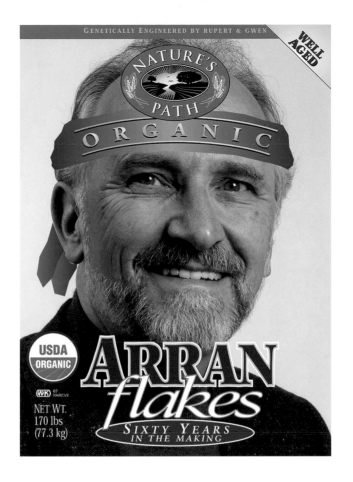

Beyond the five major goals (see page 161), our sustainability projects have grown internally to touch all aspects of the business. Each year, all new team members take our "sustainability 101" training, and every department has goals and projects aimed at achieving our ambitious waste and Climate Smart goals. Below are some of the many ways we care for people as well as planet.

Nurturing the Team—In addition to nurturing programs that have consistently earned Nature's Path recognition as a top employer in BC and Canada, starting in 2004 we expanded our health and wellness programs to include annual biometric testing for all team members, so they can get a snapshot of their health. We continue to offer our "Get Fit" dollars, where all team members receive annual funding

they can use to pay for gym memberships, equipment, sport activities, 5k runs, marathons . . . pretty much anything that helps motivate them to stay in shape. Our Richmond and Sussex facilities have onsite gyms (we are looking to add this to Blaine in expansion plans!) and we are constantly coming up with new ways to support and promote healthy lifestyles. In 2014, we focused more on developing a win-win maternity leave policy and addressing stress and work-life balance, with the addition of a meditation room in our Richmond home office and a new wellness area in Blaine.

Arjan, having just unearthed a handful of onions.

Fair Trade—Since 2012, Nature's Path has significantly increased our support of Fair Trade products. Small producers in developing nations are often at the mercy of large corporations that put profit before people. Fair Trade certification is a rigorous third-party verification standard ensuring that the producers of food are compensated fairly and provided access to a healthy work environment. We have been purchasing Fair Trade cocoa products since 2011, but in 2012 we completed our first Sustainable Supply Chain review in which we talked to each of our suppliers (big and small) to find out what they were doing around sustainability. We discovered that with a few adjustments, we could greatly increase our purchase of Fair Trade items. We were able to launch four Fair Trade certified toaster pastries and North America's first Fair Trade certified granola. All of our cocoa is now Fair Trade (although we haven't put that claim on all packaging yet), and we moved to 100 percent Fair Trade chocolate sources in 2014. We also purchase Fair Trade sugar, spices, coconut and vanilla for some of our products. Where possible, and where we feel we can make the most impact, we continue to expand our support of certified Fair Trade products.

Saving Energy—Although we are over 90 percent there, the goal for Nature's Path is to be zero waste to landfill by the end of 2015 and carbon neutral by 2020. Many companies have adopted green policies because, ultimately, they save energy, streamline manufacturing and end up not only helping reduce environmental impact but saving everybody money in the long run. The team has made such headway that Nature's Path has been awarded Top Green Business in BC and in Canada in 2009 and each year from 2011 to 2015.

A testament to the team is that we have so many positive things to say on our packages that there's no space left to add more information. A good friend with three young children called me up a couple of years ago wondering whether we used the "good" type of plastic, as some other companies were advertising this as a featured claim. I had full faith in whatever the Nature's Path team does, however . . . I rang up Jyoti and asked her whether we were using the "good" plastic. "Of course!" she

replied. "We've used it from the beginning." "Well, why don't we add that label to the packaging, then?" I asked. "No space," she confirmed.

After the opening of the Blaine plant, a granola line was introduced, with Hemp Plus® granola a key player.

HEMPTATION

In the 1990s, hemp was still a dirty word. The sale of hulled hemp seed was banned in the US and shipments were being seized. While Arran loved the nutritional benefits of hemp seed, he was wary of incorporating it into Nature's Path products. Unlike a certain US president, Arran did inhale in his teens, but since 1964 he has never consumed alcohol or recreational drugs; he was concerned that uneducated consumers would mistakenly think Nature's Path was advocating drug use. He had good reason for concern, as there was a lot of misinformation floating around. As an example, the later Hemp Plus® Granola Bars were featured on a Japanese TV show that wrongly suggested that people could get "stoned" off our food.

We have had to educate both customers and the government about the value of hemp seed and its distinction from marijuana. The non-psychoactive forms of hemp are as nutritious and compelling a food supplement as flax, especially for those who cannot consume fish oils. Hulled hemp seed contains beneficial omega-3 and -6 fats, with taste-bud-pleasing—and no mind-altering—effects. As an interesting factoid,

NATURE'S PATH IS A GROWING FAMILY ENTERPRISE whose mission for over 20 years has been to nurture the earth while improving the health and happiness of its people. Now, our popular wholesome cereals have been transformed into a new array of deliciously chewy granola bars available in five mouthwatering flavors. These certified organic bars are loaded with heart-healthy organic oats and give you one complete serving of whole grain. From the sweet goodness of raisins, apricots and cranberries to the crunchy yumminess of pumpkin seeds and peanuts, it's amazing how a snack so nutritious can taste so good. Enjoy!

Arran, founder of Nature's Path holding a fresh loaf of organic whole-grain bread in LifeStream Natural Foods Store, 1971.

Always cherish nature.
— Gwen Stephens, pioneering organic farmer and mother of Arran, Nature's Path founder.

ORGANIC
Nurturing people, nature and spirit.

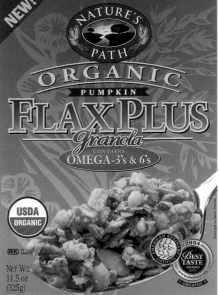

the original constitution of the United States was printed on hemp paper; hemp was also grown by George Washington and Thomas Jefferson!

When we first launched Hemp Plus® granola, there were no cereal companies our size incorporating the nutritious hemp seeds in granola. It was a tough act when scared buyers were returning product. Hemp advocacy and education has been key to hemp's success. Arjan recalls that, when the hemp trade association was lobbying for the rights of industrial hemp as a legitimate food, Nature's Path was key in bringing the fight to the Supreme Court. In 2009, the US Industrial Hemp Farming Act passed, making industrial hemp cultivation legal.

The simpler path would have been to discontinue Hemp Plus®, but the team held to its determined "hemp vision" and eventually prevailed. And to sweeten the victory even further, during the time we were losing shelf space due to product returns, Arran developed Pumpkin Flax Plus® granola. Born of necessity, Pumpkin Flax Plus® turned into another powerhouse. Hemp Plus® remains popular today.

So much of what Nature's Path does is education, from teaching consumers the benefits of organic foods to the benefits of ancient grains and seeds. As with the ongoing battle to label GMOS in North America, Nature's Path will not hesitate to stand its ground in support of what is right, just, fair and true. At the cutting edge of so many food and farming revolutions, Nature's Path not only provides delicious and nutritious products, we have been gradually changing the way people eat. For the better.

Robyn O'Brien.

GROWING GMO AWARENESS

When you look your little ones in the eye, you will find your voice and take a stand for them. We must have the courage to stand up for them, whatever the odds or however powerful the opposition might be.

— ROBYN O'BRIEN, author, concerned mother and the "Erin Brockovich of Food"

Arran was invited to become a founding member of the non-profit Non-GMO Project in the mid-2000s, when lawmakers in North America appeared determined to ignore compelling

concerns about this technology. Concerned consumers were outraged (as they are today) that GMOs were being allowed into our food supply without their knowledge or consent. As presidential campaign promises in the US to label GMOs turned from battle cries to inaudible whispers, the onus was on determined citizens and visionary organizations to make change. As Gandhi says, "Be the change you wish to see in the world." With backlash against GMOs rising, people were organizing. The non-profit Non-GMO Project grew out of this non-violent resistance, people coming together to preserve and build a non-GMO food supply, educate consumers and provide verification (the "Non-GMO Project Verified" seal) for non-GMO products.

For Nature's Path, this verification means that every load of "at risk" raw organic materials we receive, such as corn, canola

and soy, is tested at source and shipped to us only if it meets a threshold of at least 99.1 percent genetic purity. The label was first used on our packaging in 2011 and, as with organic certification, Nature's Path was a first on many fronts with Non-GMO Project verification. While the organic label implies that a food was grown without GMOs, having both seals on our products is assurance to our customers and increases awareness of GMOs. Arran is quick to warn that:

> The Non-GMO verification seal does NOT mean that the product has been grown without toxic agricultural practices, *unless* that product is also certified organic. It just means that it is not genetically engineered. That is why, for food safety, organic is always your gold seal of quality.

ARJAN AND THE TOASTER PASTRY PLANT

My baby brother, Arjan, at 6 feet 2 inches, now towers over us all. From the trials of teenhood emerged an incredibly balanced, intelligent, loving, caring and business-minded individual. Along with my father, Arjan possibly shares our family's greenest thumb (my husband, Pascal, is becoming a close contender). A passionate gardener, he gives free organic gardening classes. Like my father, Arjan is a talented painter but funnels his creative passions into Nature's Path products. In a CBC interview he confessed, "I dream in cereal."

A lover of history, Arjan got his BA in history from Queens University in 2003. Accepted into the joint law and business program at the Illinois Institute of Technology's Kent and Stuart schools, Arjan applied himself to MBA studies in 2005–6, and started the law portion at the Kent School. However, he felt a mighty tug from our dad and from the ever-growing Nature's Path. The company just couldn't halt its meteoric rise to wait for Arjan to get his law degree.

In 2006, at the age of 26, Arjan demonstrated his dedication, hard work and perseverance by setting up North America's first organic toaster pastry plant in Mississauga, Ontario. He was so passionate and eager to prove his mettle that he ended up following his father's example and bringing a sleeping bag into an empty factory office during the renovations. Arjan not only opened the plant on time and under budget, he assembled an amazing team, including the late Bruce Pratt. Pratt's daughter shared with us that her father's time working with Arjan and Nature's Path was the most meaningful experience in his career.

Arjan with Toaster Pastries.

The Toaster Pastries have done well. A September 2014 article in the *Wall Street Journal* names Nature's Path's Toaster Pastries as a healthy alternative to Pop-Tarts. Arjan is quoted as saying that, while Nature's Path pastries are still high in sugar, they appeal to people looking to avoid artificial ingredients like dyes. They are also certified organic, some with additional Fair Trade ingredients, all of which are grown and processed without toxic pesticides and herbicides.

The Nature's Path team has gone from strength to strength since Arjan came on as Director of Strategy and later moved to Executive VP of Sales and Marketing. In the first decade of this new millennium, Arjan more than demonstrated his strong leadership and vision.

Markus Schramm with Arran's homegrown pumpkins.

MANNA MOVES MARVELOUSLY

In this beautiful, ever-turning circle of life, my sister Shanti and my Bavarian-born brother-in-law Markus acquired Manna from Nature's Path in 2008. Like all our family members, Markus is a proven hard-worker with stellar experience and qualifications. He became an industrial engineer and trained at Mercedes-Benz in Germany before moving to Chicago in the mid-1990s. Nature's Path and Manna remain intimately related, with Nature's Path distributing Manna Organics sprouted Manna Bread® throughout North America. Shanti explains:

Early in 2008, my parents offered us the opportunity to acquire the Manna division of Nature's Path. It seemed perfect, with Markus's background as an industrial engineer and my business experience. Eager to embark on a new journey we took up the challenge, fixed up a warehouse in the Chicagoland region and started a commercial bakery and food kitchen. Soon after, we launched sourdough and gluten-free breads and nut butters—always organic, kosher and vegan. With the help of our dedicated and hard-working staff, we've grown into an independent, entrepreneurial and nimble food company with big plans for the future.

Markus and Shanti revamped Manna Bread® and put their own stamp on it. They have also developed a complementary range of fantastic certified organic products, many of which include

Shanti after completing a half-marathon in 2014.

sprouted and functional foods. Markus is not the first in his family to display a passion for food. His mother has published several vegetarian cookbooks in Germany. "I was always drawn to foods that are made with only a few ingredients, are delicious and replenish the system, such as sprouted and fermented foods," says Markus. Reflecting on his last eight years as a "baker," Markus says, with his endearing belly laugh, "It is easier to use the dough than to make the dough." Manna's sprouted nut butters and kale chips have become family favourites and we can't wait to taste what will come next.

Dag, our Organic Programs Manager: "Organic agriculture sets out to mimic nature."

SECURING LAND FOR THE FUTURE

Sadly, many organic farms are lost when farmers retire and have no one to take over. As demand for Nature's Path's products continues to grow, we want not only to secure more supply, but to ensure that farmland goes into the right hands. To this end, Dag Falck joined us as Organic Programs Manager in 2003. Originally from Norway, Dag studied agronomy at university and was taken aback by "modern" chemical and industrialized farming back in the 1970s. Rejecting that career trajectory, he consciously decided to dedicate his life to the organic calling. Dag speaks to the inspiration he found out in the fields:

Garth Glass, from our Saskatchewan Fox Valley family farm partner.

In the early 1990s as the first organic inspector on Vancouver Island, what drew me—and the early farmers—to organic was that this was a way to be active contributors to humanity; after all, what better way than to grow healthy food? We wanted to do this in a way that not only provided healthy, toxin-free food, but also nurtured the soil and the environment around the farms in a way that truly leads to sustainable, healthy ecosystems and food sources for future generations. You see, organic is about more than just what is *not* used (synthetic pesticides and fertilizers, etc.). It is a positive system for regenerating soil fertility, growing food in a way that actually builds healthy soil rather than depletes it.

With his lifetime of experience, Dag will patiently, logically explain to you that organic agriculture can result in equal or

A child from our Fox Valley family farm en route to school.

Ray and Holly Peterson, from our family farm in Saskatchewan.

higher yields than conventional or GMO agriculture (which depend on perfect conditions and the input of massive fossil fuel resources). Independent study after study confirms this. For a reference, the Rodale Institute has published over 35 years of consecutive farm systems trials and have found that organic methods even *outperform* "conventional," especially in drought conditions. We can feed the world without synthetic chemical pesticides, herbicides, fungicides—and as a matter of fact, there is no other way to do it, as we will at some point exhaust the "crutch" of fossil fuel inputs.

In 2008, with my parents' vision and Dag's wisdom and intimate agricultural knowledge, we secured almost 2,900 acres of fertile Canadian prairie land for organic cultivation. And we rejoiced. We give praise and thanks that we were able to save this precious tract of land for sustainable farming. Organics is the way

to purify ourselves, the soil, the air and our waterways. In a world where valuable farmland soil is threatened by development, dams and unsustainable agriculture, our whole team was immensely proud of this commitment to return to the soil and invest in it, for the future.

Typical grain crops grown on our land include oats, spelt, rye, soft white wheat, winter wheat and kamut®. Rotational crops we grow to add diversity and nutrition to the soil include lentils, peas, chickling vetch, sweet clover and alfalfa. Experimental crops include red fife, buckwheat and camelina. In a beautiful twist at this time of family farms being lost, one of our successful organic farmers was able to bring their son back to the farm from the oil and gas industry. Like us, they are in this for the long term, for future generations.

THE COMPASSIONATE DIET

Arran, along with Eliot Jay Rosen, authored his second book, *The Compassionate Diet: How What You Eat Can Change Your Life and Save the Planet* (Rodale). On the book's back cover, John Mackey, co-founder and CEO of Whole Foods Market (and a vegan), says:

Arran Stephens has long been at the forefront of the natural foods and vegetarian movements in North America. *The Compassionate Diet* persuasively advocates choosing a plant-centered diet rather than an animal-foods diet from a completely holistic perspective. I especially appreciate the book's extensive coverage of the spiritual aspects of dietary choice, which most of the books and essays in the important conversation about industrial food systems and diet tend to ignore.

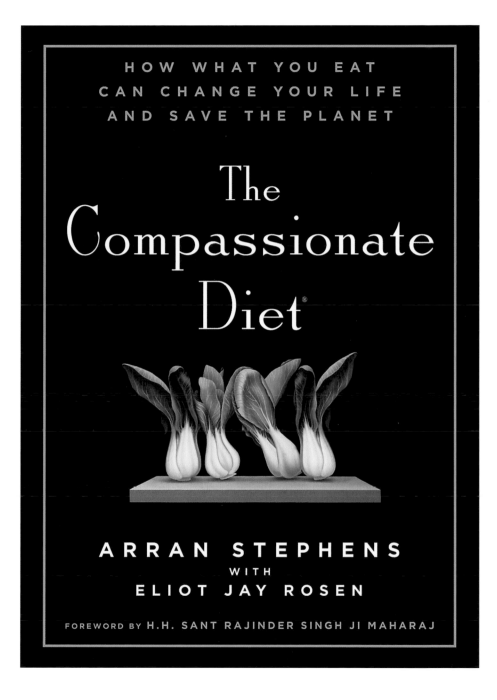

Team member Maria at our Eat Well, Do Good Foodraiser.

EAT WELL, DO GOOD

After hearing the Dalai Lama speak in Vancouver in 2008 and 2009, Arran was up to his ears in the word "compassion." Typical of my dad, he didn't want to talk about it; he wanted to put that compassion into action and, in 2009, he founded the first annual Eat Well, Do Good event, raising funds for the food bank.

The premise is simple: give away delicious free food and encourage recipients to contribute to the food bank. It seems that, to inspire others to give, we must also give. Like when we hosted the free holiday dinners at Woodlands, the Eat Well, Do Good foodraiser brings our Nature's Path family together with the goal of sharing with others less fortunate. This has turned into an annual, multi-city event, and only promises to grow as new partners join us in sharing their compassion with the hungry. To date, the Compassion into Action Eat Well, Do Good events have raised over $600,000, in food and cash, for local food banks.

The Glass "farm hero" family from one of our Saskatchewan farms.

WISCONSIN WISHES

Each of the last two decades of the 20th century saw the building of a new manufacturing plant. The end of the first decade of the new millennium continued that trend. Ratana emphasizes that the tale of Nature's Path's success is one of steady growth, rewarding diligence, care and trust. I've often heard her say, "Our success is not overnight. This is not some dotcom or high-growth technology business." Arran adds, "there are no quick fixes or get-rich-quick schemes, although if you work hard and diligently for 15 to 20 years, then suddenly people call you an overnight success!"

Like many businesses, Nature's Path experienced a minor setback in 2008 due to the global financial crisis. However, by the end of the decade, a new 230,000-square-foot food-grade facility in Sussex, Wisconsin, was up and running. In the heart of American cheese land, close to our grain suppliers and centrally located for strategic distribution, our Wisconsin plant is another win-win for us, and one for the small town of Sussex too. Here's what Arran said about it at the time to William Shurtleff, for his book, *History of Soybeans and Soyfoods in Canada:*

[The new Wisconsin plant] will significantly reduce miles traveled. For example, most of our production currently takes place in the Pacific Northwest, but half of our business is east of the Rockies. Much of our grain supply comes from east of the Rockies. By locating an additional plant in the middle of the Grain Belt, we can more cost effectively

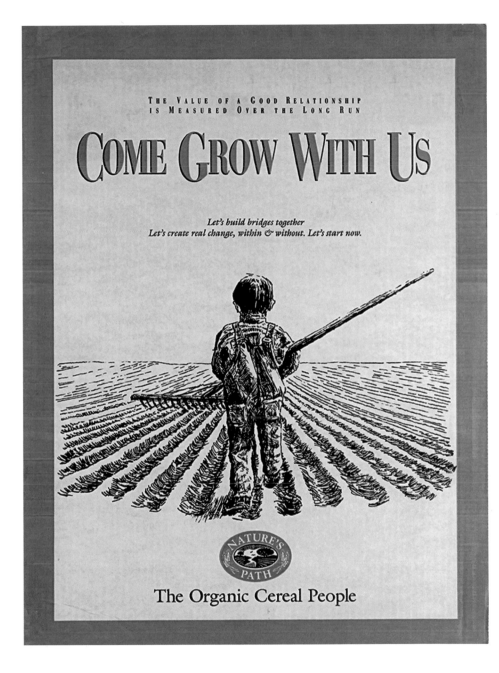

Aerial view of our 230,000-square-foot plant in Sussex, Wisconsin.

Hairnet, check, protective coat, check, then a glimpse of the packaging machinery.
BELOW: Dawn breaking at one of our Saskatchewan farms.

produce and cater to all markets east of the Rockies. The freight savings alone will be in the millions annually. With the soaring costs of the fossil fuel economy, we have to do everything to reduce energy consumption and move as quickly as possible to renewable, greener energy.

I can't think of anything more creative than Nature's Path, and it's a lot of fun, most of the time. The dynamic organization of people, the latest technology and production engineering, the excitement of moving a new concept into the marketplace and the creation of employment is satisfying. Behind each organic product is a chain supporting sustainable farming, and in front is a human being enjoying its flavour, which then becomes a part of their well-being. It's a microcosm of the cycle of life.

— ARRAN

ABOVE: Nature's Path Sussex team.   BELOW: Nature's Path Blaine team.

ABOVE: Nature's Path Que Pasa team.   BELOW: Nature's Path Richmond and Sales team.

Dear Nature's Path Foods,

I love your Leapin'Lemur peanut butter & chocolate cereal! We order several boxes every day. Since our dad can't have Gluten, and your cereal is Gluten Free, we're sure loyal customers. I hope you sell this for years to come.

Yours, Kai

2010–2015

FIELDS OF DREAMS

Life is a song, sing it;

Life is a game, play it;

Life is a challenge, meet it;

Life is a dream, realize it;

Life is a sacrifice, offer it;

Life is love, enjoy it.

— RATANA at the "Leading
Moms" event, October 3, 2012

A family shot around Mamma Bear from our Eat Well, Do Good Foodraiser.

Nature's Path receives about 50 offers to sell out per year. Arran describes them as "offers that would make your head spin." Arjan says, "if our goal was only to sell cereal and snacks, we probably wouldn't be here." When considering these offers, Arran and Ratana ask, "How would this benefit our lives and our children? Would it add to their character? Would it be of benefit to our team? We don't think so. We earn enough from Nature's Path for our needs and for various causes that we support. By selling, we'd lose control over the course of this dynamic vehicle of beneficial change. We're aware of our responsibilities. Those 50 offers go into the round file! We even say on our website, so as not to waste anyone's time, 'No part of Nature's Path is for sale.'"

The last four years have been an incredible roller-coaster ride for our family. Where to begin? The highs were my brother Arjan and sister Jyoti getting married to wonderful spouses (Rimjhim and Alex) and having babies. The lows have been health challenges, which we have thankfully surmounted. We livers walk with gratitude, our cups overflowing, savouring the moments of being healthy, alive and pain-free. A higher purpose infuses our lives, along with immense drive to continue along this path of change.

Dad says, "So long as we are given life, let it be fruitful, serviceful and loving." To celebrate life and organic farming, Dad and I recorded Grandpa Rupert's song "This Earth Is Ours" on YouTube and took a photo dressed up as the iconic couple from the painting *American Gothic*. Given the hand gestures, I call this picture Bollywood American Gothic.

WISCONSIN WINS

With our earlier plants maxed out, the Wisconsin plant has taken over several production lines during the last five years. We're now producing in earnest after the bumpy start typical of most new endeavours. Because of the capacity of Sussex, we have room to grow, yet past experience suggests we could max out again before we know it. In fact, at the end of 2014 we were already considering whether, and how much, to expand Sussex!

EVERY DAY IS EARTH DAY!

Earth Day Open Letter

On this Earth Day, we give thanks to the Earth, our Mother, and to the
Creative Spirit, our Father. We give thanks to you, our beloved Customers
for believing in and supporting Nature's Path and what we stand for:
good wholesome healing food, food which is good for the planet,
good for people, for animals, for farmers and all living things.
We give thanks for Light and Love, Peace and Beauty.
May it heal, spread and overcome the dark, the forlorn, the hungry,
the pain and the forgotten. We give thanks to the hundreds of
valued team members at Nature's Path.

There is a parable about the Earth, which we'd like to share:
Once, the Earth was asked how She could support the weight of the mountains,
the land, the oceans, the peoples, the animals, the birds and fishes.
How could she possibly withstand the occasional famine, war,
bloodshed and poverty? How could she bear such a burden?

And the Earth replied, "I can stand any burden, except an ungrateful heart."

Love to you all,

Arran & Ratana

Arran & Ratana Stephens

Nature's Path Foods Inc. 9100 Van Horne Way, Richmond, BC Canada V6X 1W3 | Tel 604.248.8777 Fax 604.248.8760 | www.naturespath.com

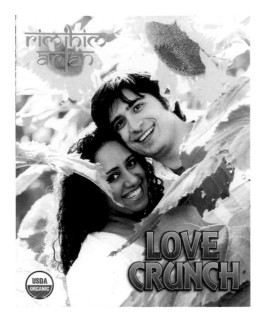

LOVE CRUNCH

My brother Arjan, in a sweet and totally unexpected way, fell in love with Rimjhim. Trained as a medical doctor, Rimjhim has a passion for nutrition and meditation. Together, the loving couple created Love Crunch granola:

While planning our 2010 wedding, we wanted to do something personal and memorable for our guests as a thank you for participating in our Experience Giving Project where, in lieu of traditional wedding presents, our guests volunteered their time to those in need. Together, and with the support of our amazing team, we created Love Crunch, a premium and sustainable blend of granola with dark chocolate and red berries.

After the wedding, we were constantly asked if we had more Love Crunch and if it were available in stores. We thought, why not? We wanted to keep the original concept of giving in mind and created the Bite for Bite program, which donated a bag of Love Crunch to a food bank for each bag sold. Nature's Path has since given millions of dollars and bags to the hungry and has extended the granola into a delicious line!

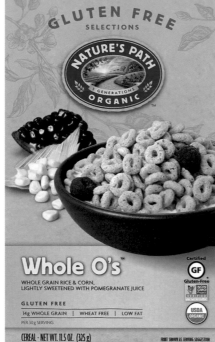

practices. The result is a brand that not only represents food at its best but which retains a position of "relevance" to consumers' everyday lives and profitability for its retail partners.

— DR. KENNETH WONG, Distinguished Professor of Marketing, Queen's School of Business

REBRANDING FOR PRODUCT UNITY

Nature's Path was a trailblazer in the marketing of organic foods, but not for the reason one might first expect. Yes, it was one of the first to aggressively promote—on an international scale—a branded organic line. However, of greater significance is what the brand represented: a combination of a good tasting, nutritional product that was environmentally minded in BOTH its products and the processes used to produce and distribute them.

Most [companies], organic or otherwise, would delight in achieving any one of those associations, let alone all three. In addition, Nature's Path has shown a consistent pattern of innovation in its flavours, product forms and business

Under Arjan's capable direction in 2011–12, Nature's Path saw the first significant change to the box designs since the Kens Koo and McCormick in the early 1990s. Arjan says in an interview with Grocery Headquarters in 2011, "We thought it was time to bring them all together under one approachable design that reflects our long-term commitment to taste, health and sustainability." With so many products and identities under the Nature's Path umbrella, the idea was to relate them more closely to each other. Arjan says, "Our brand identity was so diffuse and diluted that many people didn't realize Nature's Path was the maker of the Optimum cereals, just to give an example."

The design team worked diligently to come up with a new theme. Creative Director Jeff Deweerd has led the team for over a decade, shepherding major packaging developments that have garnered multiple awards. Of the recent redesign, Arjan says, "The 'craft' colour theme brings our sustainability message to the forefront while the vines and fruit images in the background remind people that they are purchasing ultimately on the basis of taste. After all, if our products didn't taste good, we'd not be here after 30 years."

Over the past few years, the Nature's Path family has watched Arjan come into his own. In 2012, at the age of 31, Arjan was recognized by *Business in Vancouver* with a "Forty Under 40" award, which celebrates his "excellence in business, judgment, leadership and community contribution."

GARDENS OF EATING

Arran is an incurable gardener. My dad gardened so much and so naturally when we were growing up that, when I went to other kids' homes, I was confused. Where did they put their compost? Why didn't they have fresh blueberries to pick off their mulched bushes in the late summer? Their dads would be playing golf while my dad was turning the soil! In recent years, Arran gleefully added "garden-keeper" to his business card, in addition to co-founder and CEO.

Inspired perhaps by Johnny Appleseed, Arran sows gardens wherever he goes. He even turned the back of the parking lot at Nature's Path's headquarters into a thriving garden. My mom, feeling his absence once, got a little irritated: "Why don't you hire a gardener to do the heavy lifting?" Of course, my dad gently refused. We draw sustenance and energy from the Earth. We recently watched a beautiful film about the practice of "earthing," called *Grounded*. The irrefutable premise is that the Earth actually heals. A healthy soil substrate is *alive* and we are connected in symphony, from microbes, energies, nutrients, roots and plants under foot to the oxygen-laden air we inhale outside, surrounded by nature. We often walk barefoot in our gardens and feel the healing Earth energies coming up through our feet, legs and hands.

The start of our Richmond home office garden in the back of the parking lot.

The same garden in its first year.

Team members regularly come out to the Nature's Path garden to enjoy the scenery, pick weeds, nourish the soil, plant the beds and reinforce a vital connection to nature in the city. We're also taking gardening up in the world, with an experimental green roof on the Nature's Path home office. Only by learning and making "mistakes" with gardening can we begin to understand the principles of organic soil-nurturing. For example, in our little garden at home, we once forgot to add compost to a section. Lo and behold, the beans planted there didn't grow half as big as the others. Arjan nurtures not only the Nature's Path garden but also the garden at the SOS Eco-Centre in Richmond. He told me he believes that the popular urban gardening phenomenon is

a revolution that will do so much to change the world. Not only does it put delicious, home-grown food on the table, it bonds us with nature.

Arran and Ratana's home garden is both a showplace and a provider of hundreds of pounds of vegetables and fruits, which they mostly give away to charity, neighbours and friends. It has been featured in *Organic Gardening* magazine and amazes all who are lucky enough to walk through its cornucopia of bountiful delights. Arran now keeps six beehives, plus native mason and bumble bees. One of his favourite creatures is the pollinating hummingbird moth. Yes, as nature and nurture intended.

THIS PAGE AND OPPOSITE LEFT SIDE: Team members tending to the Richmond home office garden.

In this garden section, teeming with vibrancy, fellowship and life, we want to honour our former team member, Alfonso Crescenzo (1970–2014), VP Operations (pictured above, right). Jyoti writes: "Alfonso was a collaborator, a storyteller, a push-up champion, an astute professional and a dedicated family man. He was far too young. I am proud of the mark he left on our family and our company, and he will forever be in our hearts."

Arjan and Jyoti in the Richmond home office garden.

GARDENS FOR GOOD

Around 2008–09, Nature's Path began to bestow grants to community gardens, an initiative we are pleased to see is now sprouting all over North America. This initiative began as a partnership with *Organic Gardening* magazine when we donated rainwater catchments to community gardens. The initiative later transformed into Gardens for Good, which gives three $15,000 grants a year to different deserving community gardens. Jyoti explains:

As we focus on feeding communities, we have two areas of focus. Firstly, we support the food banks, which play an important role in helping families with immediate needs to feed themselves. Secondly, we support the creation of community gardens through Gardens for Good, which is a longer-term solution. Since our first garden in 2010, we have helped raise several community gardens across North America that have helped create greater community food security.

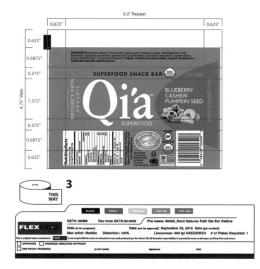

Chia field.

QI'A

Qi'a is a new favourite. Having spent so many years in Europe, living a different "flavour profile," I was pleased as punch to have a new no-sugar variety of cereal. Our fruit-juice-sweetened corn flakes are awesome as are our lines of puffed cereals with no sugar. We currently have dozens of different products with low or no sugar at all. Qi'a has ratcheted superfoods up to the next level while remaining true to our cutting-edge healthy food message launched by the original Sprouted Manna products.

Our higher purpose with Qi'a is to provide a pure, unprocessed superfood that anybody can eat, whether a struggling diabetic, a celiac sufferer or an Olympic athlete in training. Qi'a contains chia seeds, buckwheat and hemp. Its name combines the seed name "chia" with "Qi," the word for vital energy in the Chinese tradition. Arjan is pleased to announce, "Qi'a is the most successful product launch in Nature's Path history."

One of five new Qi'a bars launching at the same time as this book.

RIGHT TO KNOW

Arran first met the family of writer and visionary Dr. Vandana Shiva in 1967 in Rajpur, India. Dr. Shiva eloquently distills the conundrum of GMOs, stating, "You cannot insert a gene you took from a bacteria into a seed and call it life. You haven't created life, instead you have polluted it."

While many organic brands that have sold out have been silenced by their much-larger "conventional" new parents, Nature's Path has been at the forefront of the organic industry in standing up for GMO labeling. We have contributed significant time, money and effort to grassroots right-to-know campaigns, including California (Prop 37 in 2012), Washington State

IS THIS THE END OF REAL FOOD?

GMO OMG

a film by JEREMY SEIFERT

"Alarming"
-Variety

"Constantly provocative"
-Screen Daily

WINNER
BEST DOCUMENTARY

Nature's Path was the main funder of Jeremy Seifert's film *GMO OMG*, which won a prestigious Environmental Media Award in 2014. We also promoted the film on the back of cereal boxes.

(I-522 in 2013), Colorado (Prop 105 in 2014) and Oregon (Ballot Measure 92 in 2014). In addition, we have supported GE Free BC, federal Canadian labeling motion M-480, GMO Free LA and the Mom's March on Washington in 2011. We applaud the states of Vermont, Maine and Connecticut, which are close to giving their citizens the power to know what they're feeding themselves and their families.

We've lent our hearts and dug deep to help educate and inform North Americans that GMO food still remains unlabeled, despite the fact that people want to know what they're eating. John Fagan, one of the world's foremost experts on the myths and truths of GMOs (and co-author of the hard-hitting *GMO Myths and Truths*), acknowledges Arran's ongoing and vocal activism for the health of planet and people:

> Over the years, [Arran's] vision has been maintained and expanded as Nature's Path has "walked the talk," not only continuing to produce an ever-growing range of creative real foods, organic foods, that nourish all dimensions of life, but also continuing to challenge GMOs and industrial agriculture and to support the cause of pure, safe, healthy organic food for all. Arran and Nature's Path continue to stand as pillars of the organic movement and to take leadership in the Non-GMO Project and, recently, in several state initiatives in the US that call for labeling of GMO foods.

Letting love be her rocket fuel, Robyn O'Brien has been advocating for change within the food system ever since her child suffered an allergic reaction. She is a patriot and a self-described "unlikely food crusader." With a heart full of courage, Robyn wrote the important book, *The Unhealthy Truth,* and is at the forefront of concerned mothers working to ensure a healthy future for our children. Robyn offers her perspective:

> This movement has been built by those who came before us. The stewards of the land are the stewards of the movement.

Me and Dag the day of the successful GE FREE BC vote, fall 2013.

In no way has this stewardship been more obviously demonstrated than by Arran Stephens and the Nature's Path family. They have nurtured not only their company but also the movement the way that a grandfather nurtures a grandchild or a mother a baby—with love, discipline, resolve, patience, courage and tenacity.

Arran and Ratana, their family and the entire Nature's Path family, now and those who came before, are owed such an enormous debt of gratitude for their perseverance, love and strength to see this movement to the place it is in today. We would not be here without them, their integrity and their commitment to every aspect of our food system: farmers, the future, soil, the solidarity, the land and the love that binds it all together. And if you really listen to their words and their actions, you will hear their message for what it is: a love song, driven by the rhythm of nature and the beat of a family's heart. It is in this love that we will see this work through.

QUE PASA

When I moved back to the west coast of British Columbia after 13 years in Europe, I tried all the corn chip brands for sale and soon settled onto Que Pasa tortilla chips as my family's brand. We love those chips, and order a bag or two a week with our local organic delivery service. Just who were these amazing chip makers? They had a secret recipe I was curious about. It turns out that Que Pasa was a local family enterprise born around the same time as Nature's Path.

A few years ago, the founders began looking for a new parent for their Que Pasa baby. They were ready for retirement but didn't want to sell out to a big company. Who knows what would happen? Companies seeking only to increase the bottom line have been known to take the value and integrity of a brand and dilute the quality of the ingredients, turning "organic" into "original," or worse: "natural." Nature's Path's long-term commitment to organics and our refusal to sell out are well known. Yes, it would be hard to part with Que Pasa, but the owners were happy to entrust Que Pasa to its next stage of development. Arjan and the team believe Que Pasa can become a brand as pervasive as

Volcanic stone mill from Querétaro, Mexico, used to grind corn for Que Pasa tortilla chips. BELOW: The Glasses on our Saskatchewan farm.

Nature's Path. Mutually impressed, Que Pasa and Nature's Path were a match made in organic tortilla chip/cereal heaven.

Ready for the secret? I have to give it away, because when I walked into the chip factory floor for the first time, I almost fell down in a Stendhalian moment. In huge stainless steel vats, I saw beautiful, whole kernels of corn that had been soaked overnight the old-fashioned way. Real volcanic stones from Querétaro, Mexico, were grinding the maize, bursting in its own juices. That stunning corn mixture was then formed into circular tortillas, chopped into triangles, lightly fried and sparsely salted. I felt like I was transported to Mexico. The secret to Que Pasa's tortilla chips? Whole, organic corn kernels, including the bran and germ. Simple. Powerful. ¡Ole!

Dear Nature's Path;

We recently purchased your product Hemp Plus Granola, and we wanted to write to you, because we are completely satisfied with your product. Not only does it taste delicious; It is healthy for you!
We love that your company is certified organic, and more importantly that you label your product NON GMO. It is difficult to find foods that are labeled NON GMO, and there is absolutely no way we want to support GMO foods. We read the quote on the little tabs, and those quotes are necessary and inspire people to think outside the box. Thank you for using recycled resources to package your product.
Thank you for your excellent customer service and we will continue to support and share our oppinions about your company with our community.

♡ Sincerely
    Matt + Ashley.

Doug Crabtree and Anna Jones-Crabtree.

THE MONTANA FARMLAND PURCHASE

In the spring of 2014, Nature's Path purchased 2,769 acres in northern Montana, land planted with native grasses and untouched by chemicals for 20 years. We have partnered with OTA-award-winning nearby Vilicus Farms, run by Doug Crabtree and Anna Jones-Crabtree, true stewards of the land. These organic farmers encourage biodiversity, promoting natural processes. With healthy natural ecosystems, 21 different crops and the practice of leaving 20 percent of their land for the birds and bees ("pollinator strips"), Vilicus produces as much on 80 percent of their land as most farmers do on 100 percent. In the photos above right and opposite, you can see conservation or pollinator strips. Anna explains that these strips serve a number of purposes, including providing nesting habitat for pollinators and easier access for scouting the diversity of crops. They also reduce wind erosion and capture snowfall, keeping the soil moist and rich. In that 20 percent of land that gets included in cultivation by most other farmers, pollinators are free to feel, listen and hover.

This Montana farmland purchase is a win-win because we will all benefit from Vilicus's unique farmer apprentice program. The future of food depends not only on attracting and training new farmers to the land, but setting them up with acreage and sustainable business plans. Just as Nature's Path welcomes organic "competition" in all product categories, we would love to populate the "neighbourhood" with like-minded farmers who have collective buying power and a communal voice: farmers and friends enabling each other to shift agriculture to a sustainable, organic model.

VOX CANTATA

We want our invaluable team to have the first and last say, both figuratively and literally. To that end, the quotes on the inside covers of this book are directly from our team members. Over the years, we have grown exponentially and are honoured by the individuals who have chosen to make Nature's Path better and stronger, bringing years of vital experience and know-how.

Peter Dierx recently joined the team as VP of Operations. He shares what drew him to Nature's Path:

> I wanted in this next stage of my career to be involved in something that reflected my values. I have always been environmentally conscious, take care as to the food I eat and care deeply about the folks who work in our plants. In discussions with the entire Stephens family, I realized that these things were genuinely a part of their vision of Nature's Path. That's why I am here.

Simon Colley, our Director of Supply Chain, joined Nature's Path 12 years ago:

> I left behind a good job to come here. I was looking to have more than just a job, though. I was looking to be part of a company that was value based and had a vision to make a positive difference. I was fortunate enough to find that opportunity and have been trying to make a difference as a team member at Nature's Path ever since.

Team members Ellie (ABOVE) and Rachel (BELOW).

Team member Rachel.

Our CFO, Neil Mandleman, reflects on his first encounter with Nature's Path and how the company has changed him:

I met the family in early 2006. To be brutally honest, I came for an interview as a favour to my friend Norm. I knew the moment the interview started this was truly a family-first organization, followed by a business. The questions were very personal. It was not a normal interview, but since I am not a normal accountant, it felt fine. I saw the opportunity to work with such a family, and was hoping I would get a chance. The fact that they were pushing for my start date to be on Ratana's birthday, and I would be a gift felt really strange. But in hindsight, it all makes sense.

Over my eight years, they have not only shown me, but they have taught me the importance of family. We have laughed and we have cried (sometimes too much crying). We have argued and ultimately come to agreements. Truly a family. The fact that the grandchildren come to the office and hug me and call me uncle . . . how do you put a value to this? I would never in my career ever have thought I would want to work in such an environment. Nor did I think I could be successful in it, but I was wrong on both counts. It does work.

This place has changed me, I actually eat breakfast and do consciously stop and think of what I put in my body. I still might not do the right thing but I do think about it. And I even recycle now.

Darren Mahaffy, VP Marketing.

Arran keeps honey bees and native bee species.

Darren Mahaffy has been our VP of Marketing since 2011. He got a juicy taste of his exciting new job soon after joining the team, when he attended the Mom's March on Washington for GMO labelling.

> Before Nature's Path I had only ever worked at large, multinational companies where the only factor that mattered in business decisions was the profit impact—not the impact on people, nor the environment, nor our team members. When I came to Nature's Path I found myself making decisions based on the triple bottom line. We didn't compromise on our people for profit, and we didn't leverage the environment of future generations to satisfy our current desires. I learned how to find balance between people, planet and profit. It is a refreshingly holistic way to do business and feel like you are making a difference every day.

In 2013, Arran and Ratana won the Organic Trade Association's Organic Leadership Award. The text below is from Arran's acceptance speech, which was received with a standing ovation:

> Because of the visible stand that I and my family have taken against the artificial genetic modification of our food supply, and our fight to have GMO foods properly labeled in California and Washington State so people can make an informed decision about whether or not they wish to feed this stuff to their families, I received a tongue-in-cheek question, "Are you a packaged consumer goods company, or an activist group?" I happily answered, "Both!"
>
> Two and a half years ago, lying in the ICU ward, my life was dangling from a very slender thread, hovering somewhere in the void between life and death. It seemed then, in some strange way, that I had a choice—to go into the Beyond or

Team member Rachel (LEFT) and Gemma running with Lola (RIGHT).

stay on and complete some unfinished aspects of this existence. I chose, or so it seemed, to live on.

Having been granted a life extension, I rededicated whatever time was left to serve the Creation in some small way—on the one hand to nurture and protect the fragile earth, to help fulfill the destiny of our enterprise, Nature's Path, and ensure its smooth succession to the next generation, to be there as a loving father and husband, and on the other hand, to continue to evolve as a human and spiritual being.

In ancient times, it was said, "Honour your heavenly Father and your earthly Mother that your days may be long upon the earth, for from one mother proceeds all that lives; therefore, he that kills, kills his brother, and from him will the earthly mother pluck her quickening breast." I have always felt a kinship with this spiritual, but non-religious Father-Mother aspect of existence.

We have made many good friends over these decades, many of whom are in this hall tonight. We honour you all, we love you all. To all who are part of the burgeoning organic industry, starting with our unsung heroes—family farmers, suppliers, the hundreds of valued Nature's Path team members, wholesalers, retailers and last but not least, our millions of customers—we salute you, for without you, we wouldn't be here.

The world we all share and love is in crisis. Nature is under serious attack, and she's beginning to revolt. It's up to us to nurture and care for what is left. Our generation has made a terrible mess of polluting the nest; let us hope and pray the next generation is wiser. My dad told me, his 10-year-old son, as we hand-planted a field of corn together, to "always leave the soil better than you found it."

Organic agriculture and soil conservation is the only bulwark against this tsunami of ecological mismanagement. Because we are concerned that good organic farmland is being lost due to ageing farmers retiring with no heirs to take their place, we have begun to buy farmland, with a cooperative crop-sharing model. It is working, but with the rate of demand exceeding supply, we desperately need more young organic farmers. We are grateful to be a part of the organic solution. You are, or can also be, a part of the solution. A new, caring economy is needed. A fresh paradigm of conscious capitalism, if I may borrow the term, a new generation of idealist-entrepreneurs is much needed. There is hope, and I am an optimist. I will fight for the good of the earth so long as I live, and until the I that is my body becomes the earth, while the I that is my soul soars free from its temporal fetters to merge the lesser light with its Source in the greater Light.

Start of the Nature's Path green roof at our Richmond home office.

Some of Arran's honey bee hives.

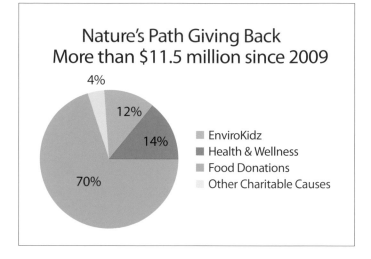

Nature's Path Giving Back
More than $11.5 million since 2009

- 4%
- 12%
- 14%
- 70%

■ EnviroKidz
■ Health & Wellness
■ Food Donations
■ Other Charitable Causes

SUSTAINABILITY SUMMARY

We publish an annual Sustainability Report and share best practices with groups including the Sustainable Food Trade Association and the Sustainability Coalition. To fulfill our goals of Earth honouring, we continually strive for the better, for the greener, for the healthier. How could we or anyone go wrong by improving the health of our Earth? We can only benefit by reducing pollution, be it via fossil fuels, pesticides or herbicides. The future is bright and it's green.

— JYOTI

In looking at what other food companies give away, we did some benchmarking. We found that most bigger food companies give more as a dollar amount (being several times our size). However, our impact is possibly more meaningful—Nature's Path gives away a higher *percentage* of our sales.

— ARJAN

GROW ORGANIC

If you value the people you work with, and respect the planet that supports you, it changes the way you do things. Organic agriculture, and an appreciation for life, is at the core of all we do.

What is it they say about one man's trash? We're always striving to reduce waste – and to turn what's left into treasure in the form of compost, green energy, and recycled materials. We've kept 91% of our waste out of landfills by composting, reusing, donating, or recycling - and we're striving for 99% by 2015.

ZERO WASTE

CLIMATE NEUTRAL

We've got a big goal – Climate Neutral by 2020 – which means we work hard to improve our carbon footprint. We reduce greenhouse gas emissions as best we can, and offset the rest to encourage green energy. Our reporting systems keep us on track, and our goal inspires us to keep improving.

Water is a precious, finite resource, so we need to use it as efficiently as possible. Choosing organic farming methods, as well as reducing – and redirecting – water waste at our plants helps us to conserve this "blue gold" for future generations.

PRESERVE WATER

ALWAYS IMPROVE

It helps to stop and look back to see how you're doing, and to share those results . We publish an annual sustainability report and work with industry groups like the Sustainable Food Trade Association and the Sustainability Coalition to share best practices (they also tell us how we're doing!)

NATURE'S PATH
3 GENERATIONS
ORGANIC

WHAT IS 'Sustainability'?

It's about meeting today's needs while ensuring a livable world for the future, and it's at the heart of all we do. After all, it's our mission to 'Leave the earth better than we found it'. That's why every decision we make must be aligned with our triple bottom line of *socially responsible, environmentally sustainable,* and *financially viable* – and why we check in to make sure we're doing our part for people and planet.

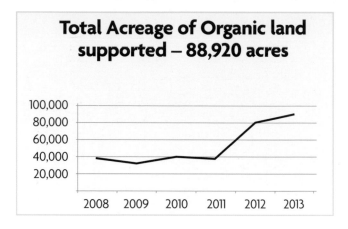

Total Acreage of Organic land supported – 88,920 acres

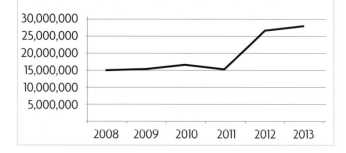

Pounds of Fertilizer Avoided – 28 million lbs annually

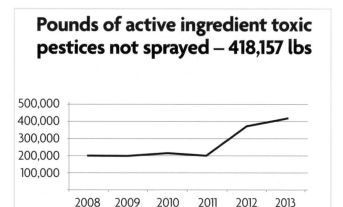

Pounds of active ingredient toxic pestices not sprayed – 418,157 lbs

TOP TEN

Though the bulk of our operations, sales and valued team members are in the US, Nature's Path has been celebrated in Canada many times. In 2004, 2005 and 2015, we were named as one of *Canada's Top 100 Employers.* We were designated one of *Canada's Greenest Employers* in 2009 and from 2011 to 2014. We've also been named one of *BC's Top 100 Employers* seven times, including 2011 to 2014. A great honour given to Nature's Path in 2015 was being named not only one of the *Canada's Top 100 Employers,* but unexpectedly making it into the top 10!

In addition to Jyoti's ground-breaking sustainability role, she took over Human Resources in 2012. Leading Employment Initiatives and Human Resources at the company, Jyoti reflects on why Nature's Path has been so generously awarded:

> Our progressive maternity leave policy, the new recognition programs, access to meditation and our great benefits, both traditional and unique—these, I believe, are what helped put our Nature's Path into the top 10. We're always getting better! To quote mom, "onward and upward!"

Pollinators come in all shapes and sizes, from bees to ants, moths, birds and mammals. Arran's favourite is the pollinator "hummingbird moth."

LOOKING OVER THE HORIZON

Having placed their stamp on Nature's Path, Arran and Ratana are now undertaking what some experts say is the ultimate test, which is transitioning the leadership of Nature's Path to the next generation and creating a legacy company for their family. It should be no surprise to anyone that an apple doesn't fall very far from the tree and that their children have many of the same traits and values that have made Arran and Ratana successful, and which, without doubt, will fuel this great organization into the future.

— ERIC S.Z. ANDREW, Senior Partner, PriceWaterhouseCoopers

Never sacrifice quality for money or for any other consideration.

Always do your best, and leave the rest.

A success is a failure that never gave up. There's no substitute for patience and persistence.

Never compromise core values and principles. Business and the market are in constant flux; VALUES never change.

Be humble.

Love your children, take care of them and help impart values. They are the future, and values are permanent.

— RATANA

In 2013, Arran made this painting from an old black and white photo of his mother, Gwen.

Arran cradling a zucchini. Arran often sends friends photos of massive veggies he grows, writing, "Look Ma! No chemicals!"

Growing up, we were always given foods that were as close to their natural state as possible. This was not always popular with us kids, but our parents had it right all along; the current movement to eating simple, unprocessed, untampered foods will drive the future of our industry and benefit generations to come. The future is bright, the future is organic!

— MARKUS and SHANTI

As a medical doctor, I always advocate for the health of my patients and now, looking through the lens of food, I have found a new avenue to do so. Over time, I hope to bring even more attention to how our choices as consumers influence what the food industry offers, and share the nutritional benefits of the organic diet.

— RIMJHIM, Health and
Nutrition Strategist since 2014

Our 2014 Montana farmland purchase brings our total organic land up to 5,640 acres. A small drop in the bucket when it comes to the millions of fertile acres in North America, but as far as we're concerned, every drop counts. As we dig deeper into Nature's Path's future, all we see is organic—organic food, organic farms and organic farmers. We see you there, too.

— DAG FALCK

I feel incredibly fortunate to work alongside my family and wonderful team here at Nature's Path. To be able to live our values through what we do, and to be given the space to be

At our sustainable palm plantation farm partner in Brazil.

creative in how the company grows and develops, is such a gift. I am also honoured that our company continues to be recognized for its work in furthering the vision set out by my parents: to be a trusted name for quality organic foods in every home—socially responsible, environmentally sustainable and financially viable.

As I look to the future, I look forward to furthering this vision together with our family and leadership team. I am hopeful that, as we grow, the food we make and the advocacy we support will continue to inspire and empower others to make values-driven choices, and that even on a small scale we can help make a positive difference in people's homes, as well as leaving the earth better than we found it.

— JYOTI

This incredible and exciting path we're on feels like the start of a marvelous journey. Being on the cutting edge of organic food development, packaging, sustainability, fair trade, socially responsible business and honouring our team members and the earth—this is our present and this is our future.

— ARJAN

This is not ours, in the ultimate sense, it is a trust from all that has passed before us. We are all standing on the shoulders of our ancestors. Yet, it is a trust loaned to us by our children.

— RATANA

Big, fundamental change always begins with an enlightened individual. That one becomes two, then four, then hundreds, then thousands, then millions. The change spreads ripples across society and across the world. Those who think an individual can't make a difference have never spent the night in a tent with a mosquito!

— ARRAN

We are the droplets of water in the tides that are turning. We are bits of stardust blowing in the winds, walking about on this precious planet. May our footprints leave no imprints. May we all shine golden with our little lights and cherish this Earth that belongs to us all.

ABOVE: My home garden. ABOVE RIGHT: A restored ecosystem at our Brazil farm partner.

NATURE'S PATH VISION:

Always leave the Earth better than we found it.

NATURE'S PATH MISSION:

To be a trusted name for quality organic foods in every home: socially responsible, environmentally sustainable and financially viable.

Paths:

Our team members are passionate about our mission and vision. Additionally, we have five core competencies that form the basis of our recruitment, training and performance-management philosophy. We strive to build a culture that is:

Performance Driven—Demonstrating initiative in supporting the goals and overall strategy of the company.

Always Improving—Commitment to LEAN, creative problem solving and continual improvement.

Team Focused—Developing a culture of high-functioning and supportive teams.

Honourable and Respectful—Contributing to a work environment that honours and respects the needs of each stakeholder.

Sustainably and Socially Conscious—Involvement in practices that decrease our negative environmental impact and increase our positive community impact.

Arran and Ratana in the Richmond home office garden.

ACKNOWLEDGEMENTS

I would like to thank my parents for creating such a company, such a vehicle of change. I thank them for not selling out, for refusing to live out the end of their days cushy, sailing azure seas on a luxurious yacht. Rather, they tend to our growing family, Nature's Path and their wonderful organic gardens. I thank them for living the example of ethical behaviour, hard work and focus. I thank them for their example of how to remain true to one's principles. I thank my father for his dedication to the soil and seed-saving. I even thank him for spitting out really good tomato seeds in the middle of dinner and putting them on a plate to cultivate later. Growing up, I really felt the "blood, sweat and tears" of business. Now, I think of business as conscious heroic choice, an opportunity born of hard work and perseverance.

Field of ripe wheat on our farm in Saskatchewan.

Restored prairie land at the Morton Arboretum.

Arran in Goldstream Park.

I thank my large family, from Uncle Godfrey (subject of my first book, *Wood Storms, Wild Canvas*) to Chaiji and my *Masis*. I thank my loving sister Shanti and siblings-in-law, Markus and Rimjhim, for their awesome words and photos. Thanks also to my brother-in-law Alex. Here's a hurrah for all the good examples, all the fun and not-so-fun times. Particular thanks to Arjan and Jyoti, who have supported every step of this book's conception and birth and have provided concrete direction for its flow and evolution.

With gratitude and appreciation to John and Ocean Robbins. You inspired my parent's generation and mine, and now you are lighting the path for upcoming leaders and food advocates. To Dr. John Fagan, Dr. Vandana Shiva, Dr. Thierry Vrain, Ken Roseboro, Robyn O'Brien, Max Goldberg, Lucy Sharratt and other

Arran in his element.

organic and non-GMO crusaders, we are honoured to have your input and words. Your dedication and expertise and continued passion for safe food is a shining example to all. Meeting Dr. Vandana Shiva inspired me to blog in an effort to emanate truth and project positive change for this blue dot we all share. We are changing the world, one meal at a time!

Much appreciation to Professor Catherine Carstairs for contributing, both by allowing me to quote freely from her extensive 2002 interview with Arran and for her own words. Likewise, Professor Ken Wong also helped to contextualize the marketing success of Nature's Path with his vast experience and scholarship. With thanks to William Shurtleff for allowing me to quote from his book, *History of Soybeans and Soyfoods in Canada*

(1831–2010). Thanks to the eco-champion David Suzuki, for allowing us to use his quote and image. May we enshrine the right to a healthy environment in our Charter of Rights!

To all the current team members, thank you for being so wonderful. We represent so many colours and faiths, backgrounds and nations. With all our diversity, we face our hearts and heads in the same direction, towards a bright future together: past the organic green horizon, up to the stars. On this caravan journey together, the team members I have gotten to know are simply some of the most talented, beautiful people in the world. Many are artists, foodies, athletes, ecofashionistas and writers in their own right. However, in putting together this book, I would like to single out Dag Falck and Jason Boyce, for their words and

Arran and Ratana's garden.

wisdom. I have to also single out Neil Mandleman for keeping it all together, keeping us all "stable" in the oxymoronic world of daily stand-up fun that is "Uncle Neil." We are a team, the sum of which is greater than our individual parts.

Thanks to Jeff Deweerd for the beautiful cover design and to him and also Brent Flink for numerous design elements. Suzanne, Noémie, Darren, Darcy, Brent, Guy, Kyla, Jenstar and Maria, thank you for your graphics, art, ideas, organization and sheer shining brilliance. Thank you to the team members who submitted compelling words and photos for the book: Dag, Jason, Jennifer, Roy, Kyle, Maria, Justine, Darren, Pegi, Candice, Simon, Neil, Chip, Kyla, Natalie, Laura, Shannon, Guy, Suzanne, Jeff,

Hormis, Marcia, Adriana, Darcy, Brent, Peter, Ellie, Sofia, Carman, Rachel, Keshni and Gemma.

Thank you to former team members who have a place in our heart forever: Maria Emmer-Aanes, Ken McCormick (the coolest-dude "Dharma bum" I ever met), John Anthony, David Neuman, Bernard Ross, Rob Wardle, Kevin Greenwood, Nicolette Mahony and Peter Tatto. I want to shout out to dear Sewa Kaur from the Woodlands daze. Alfonso Crescenzo, you were one of our MVPs and we miss you every day.

Kolin Lymworth, your story of the early Golden Lotus days really touched us all. Zio Herb Schumann, what to say but *Zehr*

Gut! Eric Andrew, where would we be without your mentoring? With thanks to our amazing editor Marial Shea and superb book designer Jan Westendorp of Kato Design and Photo; I can't believe we did this within four months. Your organization and professionalism made this book a reality. Thanks to Lana Okerlund for a professional index completed on a tight timeline. Thanks to Jorge at Friesens Press.

Over 30 photographers are acknowledged in the photo credits, but I want to single out 3: Rimjhim, Dad and Dag, you sent reams of stunning garden and nature photos, and they have made this book a delight to the eyes. Jeff Deweerd, your art-direction of our Saskatchewan family farms captured moments of beauty forever in time. Thanks also to Anna Jones-Crabtree and Doug Crabtree for photos of the Montana farmland. Thanks to Teresa Lynne, Marialena Milan and Suzanne Soldan.

Gratitude to John Mackey for inspiring a new generation of conscious capitalists and for allowing me to quote his insightful endorsement of *The Compassionate Diet.* Praise to filmmaker Jeremy Seifert for making such an important, powerful and gentle film, *GMO OMG.* Many thanks to Jeremy Douglas for your gallant coordination, and to Paul Smith for your astute and generous counsel.

I send love to soul siblings who keep my bucket of happiness full, across the continents and the fresh and salty waters of the Earth: Rita, Puri, Suromitra, Mike, Deborah, Jack, Lucy, Joseph, Rhea, Lisa, Mitra and Misty.

Trilliums in my home garden.

I honour the divine, the almighty, the inner light and the marvelous conundrum, in addition to many medical professionals who have provided me the health to write this. Drs. Chritchley, Yoshida, Scudamore, Buczkowksi and Toyota, and the too-numerous-to-mention angels (nurses). The BC Transplant Association and the Neuro-rehab at the GF Strong and Victoria General Hospitals are to thank for teaching me to use my words again.

In this second book project within a year, merci de nouveau, mon cher Pascal, and again to our talented daughters, Diya and Isha, for allowing and encouraging me to gleefully cannonball into "the Deep."

TIMELINE

1944 / Birth of Arran. When mother Gwendolyn went into labour, she was unloading sacks of potatoes.

1961 / At 17, Arran has his first poem published in *Mendicant Poetry Journal of Venice*, CA.

1963 / Arran, a self-taught artist, has first major exhibition, in a San Francisco art gallery.

1964 / Arran becomes a life-long vegetarian; Ratana is living in Uttar Pradesh.

1970 / Shanti is born; Golden Lotus is sold; start of short-lived Jyoti Importers.

1971 / LifeStream Natural Foods supermarket opens with in-store stone-milled flour operation.

1972 / Ratana takes over Mother Nature's Inn; Organic Merchants is formed; LifeStream opens Bread of Life Bakery; Arran creates Sprouted Essene® Bread with organic grains; LifeStream begins wholesale distribution across North America.

1981 / Sale of LifeStream to investors, who later sell to Nabob Coffee. Arran and Ratana open Woodlands 100-seat Vegetarian Restaurant.

1985 / First Nature's Path product, Sprouted Organic Manna Bread®, baked at Woodlands Restaurant.

1940	1950	1960	1970	1980

1957 / Goldstream Berry Paradise farm is sold; Stephens family moves to Hollywood, CA, where Rupert pursues new career as songwriter.

1966 / Arran opens East-West Gallery in West Vancouver.

1967 / Arran spends seven months in India; returns to Vancouver to open Canada's first vegetarian restaurant, the Golden Lotus, with $7 and a $1,500 loan.

1969 / Arran and Ratana meet and marry in Delhi, India, and return to Canada.

1974 / LifeStream opens large organic baking and processing facility on Vulcan Way, Richmond.

1979 / Opening of second LifeStream store at 2582 West Broadway.

1973–81 / Births of Gurdeep, Jyoti and Arjan.

1986 / Launch of Nature's Path leavened and unleavened breads, early cereals and full range of food products; expansion to Richmond.

1987 / Nature's Path focuses on breads and cereals; all other products discontinued.

1989 / Nature's Path Sprouted Manna® Multigrain Flakes with Oatbran and Raisins Cereal named Canada's Best New Grocery Product by *Canadian Grocer*.

1990 / Nature's Path Sprouted Manna® Cereal wins Second Best New Grocery Product in the World at SIAL food show in Paris; opening of Delta plant and HQ. Organic Foods Production Act passed by US congress.

1991 / Redesign of boxes with green borders and new oval logo.

1992 / Ratana joins Nature's Path full time as COO; Heritage® Flakes and Mesa Sunrise® are launched.

1993 / LifeStream (Nabob) is purchased by Kraft; launch of Heritage® Muesli and Blueberry Muesli; Shanti finishes her BA and manages Woodlands.

1994 / Shanti marries Markus Schramm and moves to Chicago.

2000 / Launch of Optimum® and EnviroKidz®, hot cereals, waffles.

2002 / After obtaining BA from the University of Victoria, Jyoti begins full time in Marketing; Arran receives Ernst & Young's Entrepreneur of the Year 2002 Award. The USDA National Organic Standards are enacted.

Ernst & Young Entrepreneur Of The Year®

2003 / Dag Falck becomes Organic Programs Manager. Home office relocated to former LifeStream building at 9100 Van Horne Way, Richmond. Jyoti becomes Sustainability Manager. Arjan obtains BA from Queen's University.

2004 / Nature's Path is named one of Canada's Top 100 Employers for the first time; introduction of the Envirobox™, reduces environmental footprint by 10%.

2005 / Arjan earns an MBA at the Stuart School of Business (Illinois Institute of Technology); joins Nature's Path full time.

2010 / Launch of Love Crunch® premium granola, conceived by Arjan and his wife, Rimjhim.

2011 / Rebranding of logo and all products.

2012 / Launch of Qi'a®; Arjan receives *Business in Vancouver's* Top Forty under 40 award; Rodale Institute Arran and Ratana Stephens Scholarship Fund; Arjan becomes VP Sales and Marketing; Jyoti becomes Director of HR and Sustainability.

1990   **2000**   **2010**

1995 / Nature's Path buys back LifeStream from Kraft Foods. Woodlands Restaurant is sold. The Canadian government approves the first GMO canola, soy, tomatoes and potatoes.

1996 / Arran joins the OTA board, staying until 2002; LifeStream is restored to profitability; Gurdeep finishes MA at the University of Chicago and moves to Europe. GMOs enter the world food stream.

1997 / Gurdeep becomes Export Sales Manager; Arran awarded Lifetime Achievement Award by CHFA; Blaine plant breaks ground.

1999 / Opening of Blaine plant.

2006 / Arjan becomes Director of Strategy, opens 36,000-square-foot toaster pastry plant; Nature's Path named one of BC's Top Employers for the first time.

2007 / Arran becomes a founding board member of the Non-GMO Project; Jyoti receives Green MBA from Bainbridge Institute; purchase of Wisconsin plant; Jyoti awarded Burns Bog Conservation Society Award.

2008 / Shanti and Markus take over Manna; purchase of Saskatchewan farmland; Arran elected to Rodale Institute Board of Directors.

2009 / Canadian Organic Standards introduced, making the term "organic" legally mandated for the first time in Canada; Nature's Path named one of Canada's Greenest Employers for the first time; Ratana receives YWCA Women of Distinction award; Arran becomes Chair of Richmond Food Security Society, holding the post until 2014.

2013 / Que Pasa® Mexican Foods joins the NP family; Ratana awarded Top 100 Most Powerful Women in Canada; New Hope Media Hall of Legends Award; OTA Organic Leadership Award; Dag Falck elected president of the Canadian Organic Trade Association.

2014 / Purchase of Montana farmland; Rimjhim begins full-time as Health and Nutrition Strategist.

2015 / *Financial Post's* Top 10 Employers out of 76,000 entries; Nature's Path celebrates 30 years of organics.

Canada's Top 100 Employers 2014

EVOLUTION OF CORN FLAKES
(1980s to 2015)

Nature's Path packaging has morphed over the past 30 years. To follow the Corn Flakes packaging change, here are the Honey'd and Fruit Juice Corn Flakes in a row so you can see the logo and design evolution.

179

AWARDS

The Nature's Path Family is humble about their accolades; the momentum driving change is too strong for the team to rest on their laurels, let alone catalogue them. Before this book was even conceived, I suggested making a list of awards. I was politely ignored. But upon charging ahead with the writing of this book, I spoke with one person after another at the home office who, when told there were over 100 awards for leadership and products, asked me, "Are you sure you counted correctly?"

Yes, I did. The full list of accolades includes the high-profile national nods as well as plaques celebrating our support of environmental and community events, from carbon offsets to the Commonwealth Games. Here, then, is a selection of the grander awards, leaving in just a taste of the consumer awards—for the record!

2015
Canada's Top 100 Employers
Financial Post's Ten Best Companies to Work For

2014
Canada's Greenest Employers
BC's Top Employers
Food in Canada's Leadership Award for Stewardship
Canada's Top Small & Medium Employers (first year of the award)

2013
Women's Executive Network's "Canada's Most Powerful Women: Top 100" presented to Ratana Stephens in the category "Glencore Trailblazers & Trendsetters," for "true pioneers"
Canada's Greenest Employers
BC's Top Employers
Leadership Institute Leadership Award to Arran Stephens for "character, vision and impact"
New Hope Natural Media's "Hall of Legends Class of 2013"
Organic Trade Association's Organic Leadership "Growing Organic Industry Award"

2012
Business in Vancouver's Forty under 40 presented to Arjan Stephens
Canada's Greenest Employers
BC's Top Employers
Organic Center Award presented to Dag Falck for outstanding technical contributions to organic food and farming

2011
Canada's Greenest Employers
Food Lifeline recognizes Nature's Path as Top Donor for "outstanding efforts toward hunger relief"
Canada's Greenest Employer
BC's Top Employers

2011 Consumer Awards

Babble.com Top 10 Parent-Owned Companies, EnviroKidz

Cooking Light Taste Test Awards: Flax Plus Waffles

KIWI Magazine KIWI Awards: EnviroKidz Crispy Rice Bars

Men's Health 125 Best Foods for Men: Ancient Grains Granola

Natural Health Good Food Awards: SmartBran

Real Simple Granola Road Test: Flax Plus Vanilla Almond

SELF Healthy Food Awards: Optimum Blueberry Cinnamon, Flax Plus
    Waffles with Figs, Vanilla Almond Granola

Taste for Life Essentials Awards, Favorite Snack Bar: Peanut Buddy
    Granola Bars

Vegetarian Times Foodie Award, Reader's Choice Granola: Hemp Plus

Women's Health 125 Best Packaged Foods For Women: Optimum Slim

2010

Wishing for Manufacturing Awards Winners and Runner-up

Natural Products Expo West "Green Packy" Award for Responsible
    Packaging Achievement

Food Trade Sustainability Leadership Responsible Packaging
    Achievement Boston for Reduced Packaging: 100% Recycled Granola
    Bar Boxes

BC Food Processors Energy / Sustainability Award

Seattle Business Washington Manufacturing Award

2010 Consumer Awards

KIWI Magazine Best Kid's Foods: EnviroKidz

Men's Health Nutrition Award for Best Granola: Organic Pomegran Plus
    Granola with Cherries

Shape Magazine Best Snack: Pumpkin-N-Spice Granola Bar

Fitness Magazine Best in Snacks: Mmmaple Pecan Granola Bar

Good Housekeeping 50 Best Low Calorie Snacks: Sunrise Cereal

2010 Trade Awards

Mediaweek Media Plan of the Year Award

Progressive Grocer Best New Products: Sunrise Cereal

Canadian Grand Prix New Product Award: Flax Plus Maple Pecan Cereal

2009

Canada's Top 100 Employers Project: Canada's Greenest Employers

BC's Top Employers

Mehfil Award presented to Ratana Stephens for Corporate Excellence

Supermarket News Profile in Industry Excellence presented to Arjan
    Stephens

Provender Alliance "Ethical Voyager Award" for "leading the organic
    foods community with sustainability in heart and action, protecting
    the future by taking care today"

YWCA Vancouver Women of Distinction Award presented to Ratana
    Stephens for "entrepreneurship and innovation"

Canadian Grand Prix New Product Award: Organic Flax Plus® Maple
    Pecan Crunch

2009 Consumer Awards

Good Housekeeping 100 Best Convenience Foods

Today's Parent Best in the Box: Breakfast Cereals, Breads & Grains

Women's Running Best Foods for Female Runners

Clean Eating Seal of Approval

Better Nutrition Editor's Pick

ODE Magazine Organic Top 20 Granola

Organic Products Retailer Stellar Organic Award, Cereal/Breakfast Food

Fitness Magazine Healthy Food Awards, Best Cereal

Real Simple Breakfast Cereal Road Test, Best Flax; Best Puffs

RealSimple.com Healthy Kids' Snack Taste Test

Women's Health 125 Best Packaged Foods for Women

VegNews.com This Week's Must Have

Woman's World You Deserve the Best, Waffles

Organic Products Retailer Stellar Organic Award, Cereal/Breakfast Food, Original Hot Oats

Grocery Headquarters Trailblazer Award, Sunrise Cereals

2008

Business in Vancouver Top 100 Private Companies in BC

BC Food Processors Association Award for Leadership

CHFA Organics Achievement Award presented to Dag Falck

2007

BC's Top Employers

Food in Canada's Food Processor of the Year

Burns Bog Conservation Society Celebrating Women and the Spirit of the Cranes: Fledgling Chick award presented to Jyoti Stephens

Metropolis Magazine's NEXT Generation design competition runner-up award presented to Jyoti Stephens for Beeline

Canadian Health Food Association's Spotlight Award: Environmental

2006

Canada's Top 100 Employers

BC's Top Employers

Integrated Health Retailer's Top Seller Review for Top Selling Bran

2005

Canadian Health Food Association's Hall of Fame Award presented to Arran Stephens at Expo West

Heritage Honors Award for Life Long Contribution to Organics

Canada's Top 100 Employers

Canadian Choice Wholesalers Vendor of the Year

BC Export Award Top 21

Canadian Grand Prix New Product Award for Optimum™ and Rebound™ Cereals

Men's Health Nutrition Award for Optimum Power™ Breakfast

BC Organic Harvest Awards Best Bakery Product

Best New Product Award voted by consumers for Nature's Path Organic Flax Plus® Raisin Bran

Men's Health Nutrition Award for Best Instant Oatmeal: Nature's Path Flax 'n Oats

2004

Canada's Top 100 Employers

Canadian Grand Prix New Product Award for Innovation

Alive Publishing Group Bronze Award of Excellence for EnviroKidz® Gluten Free Vanilla Cookies

Soil Association Organic Food Awards Certificate of Excellence, Optimum Power™

2003

Canadian Health Food Association President's Award for "most creative exhibit of diverse health supportive products" at Expo West

Canadian Institute of Food Science and Technology CEO of the Year Award presented to Arran Stephens for "outstanding contribution to the Canadian Food Industry"

2002

Canadian Health Food Association Organics Award of Excellence for "outstanding contribution to the development and growth of the organic products sector"

Ernst and Young Entrepreneur of the Year Manufacturing Award Winner World-Canada Pacific Region presented to Arran Stephens

Entrepreneur of the Year National Citation Product Development and Marketing Excellence

Alive Publishing Group Bronze Award of Excellence for Optimum Power™ Breakfast Cereal

1999

Packaging Association of Canada Marketing Magazine Package Silver Design Award: Nature's Path Hot Cereal

Packaging Association of Canada Marketing Magazine Package Silver Design Award: Kamut® Crisp Cereal

Paperboard Packaging Council's Excellence Award for achievement in packaging

Ethics in Action Awards Recognizing Leadership in Corporate Social Responsibility and Ongoing Social Responsibility Business Nominee

Pro Organic's Heritage Award Honour presented to Arran Stephens for his "life long contribution to organics"

1997

Northwest Natural Foods Industry Lifetime Achievement Award presented to Arran Stephens, "for a Lifetime of contributions on the frontier" of the industry

Ethics in Action Award Nominee

1996

Business in Vancouver Million Dollar Achiever Award for "outstanding achievement in business"

1994

National Nutritional Foods Association, First Place: Cereal Flakes

1992

BC Trade Export Award

1990

Salon International D'Agroalimentaire (SIAL, Paris) World's Second Best New Grocery Product: Manna Multigrain Oatbran Flakes with Raisins

1989

Canadian Grocer magazine names Manna Multigrain Oatbran Flakes as Canada's Best New Grocery Product

Northwest Natural Foods Industry Lifetime Achievement Award presented to Arran Stephens, "for a Lifetime of contributions on the frontier" of the industry

Ethics in Action Award Nominee

APPENDIX

GMOs

I would like to thank Dr. John Fagan, Dr. Thierry Vrain, Ken Roseboro, Lucy Sharratt and Dag Falck for their valued input into this section.

When I was getting my honours bachelor's degree in biology and my masters degree in biopsychology at the University of Chicago from 1991 to 1996, the field of biology was buzzing about genetic engineering. Biologists were promising to eliminate pesticide use and create superfoods with this new technology. They would solve world hunger through their cleverness and technology. I thought it fascinating that under the guise of improving food, scientists were basically unleashing brand new species onto the planet. Many people, including my father, were dead opposed. Initially, I was trying to figure out why. Biologists and shills for the biotech industry made it all sound so rosy. Over the years, I've tried hard to understand the pros and cons of this technology. I've discovered that, despite the hype and initial promise, there are very few pros. Below, I discuss the major cons—six big problems with the use of genetically modified organisms in our food supply.

Organic farming is a way of incorporating the entire ecology, the ecosystem of a "farm," promoting pollinators, enriching the soil and looking at the whole system. The premise behind GMOs is to grow unicrops, taking one factor, the gene, and altering

the genome, without considering the whole. Biologists were attempting to fix something when nothing was broken to begin with. There is no shortage of food, but rather of distribution.

The first major problem is that GMOs cannot be grown side by side with organic crops. They are not only the furthest thing from natural (think fish DNA in a tomato) but, because they are living and capable of reproducing, they cannot be contained. Pollen from engineered crops is carried everywhere by the wind and by pollinators, including into organic fields, which are then contaminated with genetically engineered genes. Arran said in 1996, "there are no walls high enough to keep out GMOs." You cannot have a field of organic crops right next to a field of GMO crops because the wind and pollinators will spread the GMO pollen to the non-GMO organic plants. Most people have heard about the huge number of lawsuits launched by the big biotech companies against farmers. According to one account, over the last 15 years an average of one lawsuit a week has been launched against a farmer for patent infringement. How can we patent nature? Farmers affected by GMO crop contamination did not want the GMOs, did not grow them on purpose and didn't even know of the contamination until they were sued. If someone sprayed toxic paint that disrupted my farm, the sprayer would have to desist and provide restitution. However, in this twisted world of big biotech business, it is the persecuted who lose out.

Secondly, GMOs use a lot of pesticides, which are incompatible with the organic system of agriculture. Most people are shocked to learn that GMOs have not decreased pesticide use despite biotech claims that they do so. In fact, 1.5 million tons of pesticides and herbicides were sprayed on US crops in the mid-1990s. The amount is increasing exponentially. A study by Charles Benbrook, PhD, research professor at the Center for Sustaining Agriculture and Natural Resources at Washington State University, found that pesticide use has increased by 404 million pounds since GM crops were first planted in 1996.

The sad fact is that over 90 percent of North American GMO crops are designed to be resistant to the herbicide glyphosate (which is also patented as an antibiotic and kills the bacteria that are so important to soil fertility). In private correspondence with me, Dr. Thierry Vrain explained that glyphosate was originally patented as an industrial pipe cleaner. This chemical was discovered to kill bacteria, plants and fungi, and in 1974 it was purchased and patented into the widely used, best-selling herbicide which will not be named. At this time, explains Dr. Vrain, "it was assumed to be completely safe to humans because of its mode of action to kill plants." But, as Dr. Vrain said in a recent lecture, "imagine a chemical contaminant that would destroy all vitamins in the food. Vitamins are all co-factors of enzyme proteins. Glyphosate does not affect vitamins at all, but it does deplete the food of minerals. Minerals in our food are also co-factors of enzyme proteins." Glyphosate is now also patented as an antibiotic, which apparently doesn't attack our "human cells," but certainly attacks our gut bacteria via the shikimate pathway. We walk about with over 10 times more symbiotic bacterial cells than human cells. The first glyphosate-resistant crops were released in 1996 and, because these crops are sprayed, the resulting foods we consume contain "much higher residues," says Dr. Vrain.

Most GMOs are genetically modified to resist glyphosate or to express a pesticide, such as Bt corn. Genetic engineers from the world's largest chemical companies have developed strategies in the laboratory to "stack" several traits in one seed so that a single crop will be herbicide resistant in addition to expressing a pesticide. This is extreme agriculture, as far removed from organic or traditional breeding methods as one could conceive. In recent years, with overuse of pesticides and herbicides (across 395 million acres of GMO production), superweeds and superpests have proliferated to such an alarming extent that, in 2014, the US and Canada permitted resistance to 2,4-D to be genetically engineered into seeds. 2,4-D is a highly toxic component of the infamous herbicide Agent Orange, used as a biowarfare agent during the Vietnam War. According to US Department of Agriculture estimates, the use of 2,4-D could triple by 2020. GMOs have exacerbated the problems of pesticide use, not diminished them.

The third major problem with GMOs is that safety testing is inadequate to protect the health of those who might eat them. The GMO crops grown today were all approved for commercial production without any independent or long-term animal, human or environmental toxicity studies. In Canada and the US, GMO versions of crops are considered to be "substantially equivalent to conventional crops." If this is true, then why is herbicide-resistant GMO Bt corn registered with the Environmental Protection Agency as a pesticide? And, if they are considered equivalent, why are they patented? By its very definition, a patent is awarded when something is "substantially" different. Every short-term study used to "prove" their safety to regulators has been done by the very same companies selling the GMO seeds and chemicals. Every scientific study that questions or sheds doubt upon the safety of GMOs is immediately subjected to discrediting by scientists who have direct or indirect financial ties to the biotech industry. There is no scientific consensus on the safety of GMOs.

Related to this third issue is North America's failure to question biotech's data and ban GMOs, while other countries have called the same data into question and rejected GMOs. As John Fagan, PhD, writes, "shockingly, no country has done its own research

to date. All buy in to the biotech companies' own data." In North America, legislators have not questioned the data nor done independent studies on GMOs. As a consequence, we are being force-fed GMOs, without knowledge or consent, based upon studies done by the very companies that are profiting from patenting this technology, selling the seeds and countless tons of pesticides and herbicides. Consistently, over 90 percent of North Americans polled want GMOs labeled. However, lawmakers are not listening. Sixty-four countries around the world either have mandatory labeling of GMOs or ban them altogether. When I was in my twenties and living in Europe, I was invited to the UK houses of parliament in the 1990s for backroom debates on GMOs. I wasn't at all impressed with the biotech research they presented. At the time, I had a particularly keen eye for data, having conducted laboratory research myself. Fortunately for the Europeans, they were not impressed with pro-GMO research either. They limited GMO crop trials and instituted mandatory labeling of GMOs. To date in Europe, Spain is the only country where GMO seeds are used to any significant extent, and at least six EU countries forbid any cultivation of GMOs. Other countries have taken a strong stand against GMOs, even when in the midst of a national emergency. Following the Haitian earthquake, a large biotech company provided "aid" in the form of seeds, and instead of planting them, the Haitian people wisely burned those seeds, saying they were "poison."

Recently, influential countries have taken a critical position regarding GMOs. Russia has banned them, and high-level military officers in the Chinese army have pointed to imported GMO grains as a threat to national security, saying they weaken the local agricultural production capacity. In 2014, China rejected corn exports from the US worth more than $1 billion due to the presence of a GM corn variety that has not been approved in China. With the rest of the world already alerted to the failing GMO crop experiment, only now are North Americans becoming aware of this issue and taking action to implement labeling laws. Today, Canada and the United States are the only two developed nations that do not give their citizens transparency regarding what they are eating, but with the newly enlivened attention to the GMO issue, this blind spot will soon be eliminated.

The fourth major problem is that people are under the misguided impression that GMOs increase yields and consequently are "feeding the world." In fact, of the major commercially grown GMO crops (corn, soy, canola, sugar, cotton), there have been no intentional genetic modifications for increased yields. In other words, no yield-increasing traits have been inserted through genetic engineering.

A fifth major problem is that of the ethical question of patenting "life," coupled with the problem of whether gene-splicing technology is inherently safe. I'm going to avoid this discussion for this book. It is such a vast and technical discussion and can be easily researched for those who are interested. What is more concerning on a practical level is that most of the millions of acres of GMOs grown are made by only a small handful of extremely large chemical and seed corporations. These huge multinationals own the GMO seeds, the patents, the technology and the herbicides and pesticides that have to be grown concurrently with the GMOs. These corporations are able to buy

and sway public opinion, directly or indirectly fund much of the science driving GMO research and actively lobby the government. In addition, the amount of subsidies given to "conventional" food production is staggering in size compared to organics, where farmers have to pay to be certified. It boils down to a few companies patenting life and nature . . . and it's all for profit. GMOs were allowed because of the promises of "feeding the world," reducing pesticide/herbicide use, increasing yield and making "superfoods," none of which have come to pass.

This brings us to the last major problem with GMOs: they didn't do what they set out to do. GMOs haven't alleviated world hunger, they haven't decreased toxic herbicide and pesticide use, they haven't improved crop yield and they haven't delivered super-nutritious foods. Owning patents on life is not the same as providing food for the hungry. The problem of hunger is not a question of quantity but of distribution. As United Nations studies consistently report, small scale, sustainable farming is capable of solving the food shortage and promoting biodiversity at the same time. In the long run, GMOs are out-performed by organics, especially for smaller farms and during drought conditions.

Let us collectively take the knowledge we have gained over the millennia of crop-breeding. Let's wisely incorporate modern technologies, like marker-assisted selection, that protect the integrity of nature. By keeping seed biodiversity and trusting in Nature, we can heal the Earth, feed the hungry and breed wonderful new varieties of foods, at the pace of the seasons.

Harvest time at one of our Saskatchewan farms.

SOURCES

Many of the quotes of Arran are from an extensive 2002 interview by Professor Catherine Carstairs for the book *Edible Histories, Cultural Politics* (see details below).

Several of the precise dates in this book were confirmed in William Shurtleff's interview of Arran for his book *History of Soybeans and Soyfoods in Canada (1831–2010)* (see details below, under Part 4).

I interviewed the following people in person and/or in writing: Bernard Ross, John Anthony, Ken McCormick, David Neuman, Eric Andrew, Peter Tatto, Jason Boyce, Dag Falck, Arran Stephens, Ratana Stephens, Shanti Stephens Schramm, Jyoti Stephens, Arjan Stephens.

Note that for several of the early newspaper clippings quoted, I don't have the date or name of the publication.

The following sources are presented in roughly the order they are referenced in the text.

Introduction and 1944–1985 Deep Roots: Goldstream to LifeStream to Woodlands

Arran Stephens, *Journey to the Luminous* (Seattle: Elton-Wolf Publishing, 1999).

Arran Stephens, "Moth & The Flame/Viaje a lo Luminoso." 2002. Available online at arranstephens.com.

Arran Stephens, *The Compassionate Diet: What You Eat Can Change Your Life and Save the Planet* (New York: Rodale Books, 2011).

"History of Organic Farming," Wikipedia, http://en.wikipedia.org/wiki/History_of_organic_farming.

Mary V. Gold, "Organic Production/ Organic Food: Information Access Tools," http://www.nal.usda.gov/afsic/pubs/ofp/ofp.shtml (used for USDA definition of "organic").

Ron Baird, "Song-writing Success in Sight for Berry Farmer at Goldstream." (Victoria) *Daily Colonist,* February 18, 1951.

"Strawberries in October." (Victoria) *Daily Times,* October 26, 1948 (photo of young Arran eating strawberries).

Rupert Stephens, "Sawdust Is My Slave—Part One." *Good Earth Journal,* Vol 2, No 1 (April 1992). 10–14.

Rupert Stephens "Sawdust Is My Slave—Part Two" *Good Earth Journal,* Vol 2, No 2 (July 1992). 12–14.

"Picks Strawberries," (Victoria) *Daily Times,* March 1952 (photo and caption of Arran eating strawberries).

"Old Sawdust Becomes Slave of Vancouver Island Farmer," (Vancouver) *Daily Province*, June 2, 1951.

C. V. Faulknor, "Fruit Grown in Sawdust Creates Island Paradise," (Victoria) *Daily Colonist,* May 10, 1953.

Tom Leach, "Sawdust mulch catches on with B.C. gardeners," *Farm and Rake Review,* June 1953. 12.

C.V. Faulknor, "Song-Writing Sawdust Strawberry Grower," c. 1950s.

"'Sawdust Farm' is Written Up in City Paper" (local Goldstream article celebrating write-up in *Vancouver Province*), author, date and publication unknown.

William Mavor, "Sawdust, Once Top Fuel, May Prove Garden Boon," date and publication unknown.

Rupert Stephens, "Sawdust Slivers," *The Beacon,* June 12, 1952.

"Ten Year Task Ends in Success" (about creating successful farm on Goldstream, songwriting, etc.), author, date and publication unknown.

"Singing Star" (about a singer who recorded some of Grandpa Rupert's songs), publication unknown, October 5, 1951.

"A Berry Paradise in Sawdust Mulch," *The B.C. Farmer and Gardener,* May 1951.

G.E. Mortinmore, "This Week's Profile: Rupert Stephens," (Victoria) *Daily Colonist,* September 16, 1956.

Catherine Carstairs, "The Granola High: Health Food in Canada," in *Edible Histories, Cultural Politics: Towards a Canadian Food History,* ed. Franca Lacovetta, Valeria J. Korinek and Marlene Epp (Toronto: University of Toronto Press, 2012).

CROPP Cooperative Roots: The First 25 Years (Wisconsin: CROPP Cooperative, 2013).

"Lifestream's founder is at it again," author and publication unknown, December 1985.

James Barber, "All the Healthiness, None of the Sludge," *Georgia Straight,* August 5–12, 1988. 17.

John Crawford, "Vegetarian choices abound," *Vancouver Courier,* January 28, 1990.

Robin Roberts, *Mehfil* magazine, 2010. 43–46.

The Lifestream Cookbook (Richmond: Lifestream Natural Foods Ltd., first printing 1977, sixth printing August 1982).

John Mackey and Rajendra Sisodia, *Conscious Capitalism: Liberating the Heroic Spirit of Business* (Boston: Harvard Business Review Press, 2013).

Kip Tindell, Casey Shilling and Paul Keegan, *Uncontainable: How Passion, Commitment, and Conscious Capitalism Built a Business Where Everyone Thrives* (New York: Grand Central Publishing, 2014).

1985–1990 Tilling the Soil: The Birth of Nature's Path

"Organic foods pave way to success for Nature's Path," *News and Views,* Winter 1991. 9.

Ken Bell, "Serving up High Tech Cereal," *The Province,* March 25, 1991.

"Of Soil, Sprouting and Cereals," *The Heliogram,* Winter 1990–91.

Barbara McQuade, "Manna from West Coast honoured at Paris show," *Vancouver Sun,* November 7, 1990.

Catherine Fuller, "A Tale of Eight Local Business Successes," *Shared Vision,* November 1990. 8–9.

"Nature's Path Produces Winning Product," *Western Grocer,* October 1990.

"Winners of the Canadian Grocer Award for Best New Grocery Products in Canada 88/89," *Canadian Grocer,* July 1990. 11–13.

"Where the Manna Flows," *Shared Vision,* July 1990.

Canadian Health Food Industry Business Report, June/July 1990.

"New Cereal Plant and Bakery in Delta the first for B.C.," *BC Grocer,* May 1990.

Leo Mullen, "Northwest's organic Manna," *Bellingham Herald,* April 16, 1990.

Rob Klovance, "Organic foods win green consumer," *Richmond Review,* April 8, 1990.

"Success through Nutrition," *Western Grocer,* c. 1990s. 73–75.

"Selling 'rice flakes' to the Japanese," c. 1990.

Rosemary Eng, "Delta Plant Produces Breakfast of (Organic) Champions," publication unknown, c. 1990.

1990–1999 Nourishing the Soil

John Wolcott, "Nature's Path sure route to U.S. markets," *Puget Sound Business Journal,* September 16, 1991.

Ian Edwards, "Following Nature's Path," *Business in Vancouver,* October 27–November 2, 1992. 8–9.

"Organic Path Back to Nature," *Common Ground,* March 1997. 5–8.

"Rustle my Jimmies," http://www.jimmyfungus.com/2012/04/that-really-rustled-my-jimmies-complete.html.

Kie Relyea, "Organic cereal factory's on a roll," *Bellingham Herald,* July 18, 1999. E1–2.

Dean Kahn, "Nature's Path Foods breaks ground for Blaine factory," *Bellingham Herald,* c. 1997.

Justine Hunter, "Organic food enterprise grows," *Vancouver Sun,* January 26, 1999.

"Nature's Path celebrates its new home," *Northern Light,* August 12–18, 1999.

"Clean and Green," *Horizon Air* front cover, August 1991.

2000–2010 Sowing the Seeds: Into the Mainstream

Ian MacNeill, "From Tiny Seeds Do Mighty Corporations Grow," *Grocer Today,* November 2002. 8, 10.

Jennifer Hunter, "Setting up stateside," *MacLean's,* date unknown. 38.

"Entrepreneur," *Financial Post,* April 30, 2004. FP18.

"Nature's Path Completes New Plant," *Natural Foods Merchandiser,* January 19, 1999.

Justine Hunter, "Organic food enterprise grows," *Vancouver Sun,* date unknown. D1, D14.

Stephen H. Dunphy, "Economic memo," Seattletimes.com, 1999, http://www.seattletimes.com/mews/nusiness/htm198/dunp_011999.html.

"Demand for organics continues to grow," May 1999. 13, 34.

Lisa Schmidt, "Organic farming—last chance for family farm? Backlash against GM foods will push demands for organic products," *Beacon Herald,* December 18, 1999.

Bonnie Hartley, "The New World Organic Part II," *Healthy and Natural Journal,* December 1999. 86–88.

Sushil Kutty, "The New Chemical Free Diet," (Dubai) *City Times, Khaleej Times,* February 13, 2004.

Jaime Kowal, *Waking Up the West Coast: Healers and Visionaries* (Vancouver: Catalyst Publications, 2006). 72.

Shared Vision cover, "Our Heroes of Sustaintability Issue," June 2006.

"Nature's Path faces down the giants," *Baking Management,* Volume 11, Number 11, November 2007. 18–24.

Carolyn Cooper, "Going with the Grain," *Food In Canada,* January/February 2007. 42–47.

William Shurtleff and Akiko Aoyagi, *History of Soybeans and Soyfoods in Canada (1831–2010).* 2010. http://www.soyinfocenter.com/pdf/137/Cana.pdf.

Randy Shore, "Canada's first products get non-GMO certification," *Vancouver Sun,* July 2, 2010.

Willi Evans Galloway, "Reclaimed Retreat," *Organic Gardening,* April 2007.

Marty McDonald, "Nature's Path Serves up Sustainability with Cereal," *GreenBiz,* December 7, 2009, http://www.greenbiz.com/blog/2009/12/07/natures-path-serves-sustainability-cereal.

Amanda Baltazar, "One Small (Carbon) Footprint for Food Manufacturers," *Nutraceuticals World,* http://www.nutraceuticals-world.com/contents/view_online-exclusives/2009-07-01/one-small-carbon-footprint-for-food-manufacturers/.

2010–2015 Fields of Dreams

"Compassion Into Action" event announcement, https://www.food-bank.bc.ca/events/compassion-into-action-1.

"Nature's Path Invests in a Sustainable Future with Purchase of 2,760 Acres of Organic Farmland," http://us.naturespath.com/press-release/natures-path-invests-sustainable-future-purchase-2760-acres-organic-farmland.

Jane Hoback, "Companies with a Cause: Nature's Path," NewHope.com, July 29, 2010, http://newhope360.com/news-amp-analysis/companies-cause-natures-path.

Sarah Nassauer, "Amid Kale and Quinoa Pop Tarts Keep Hanging On," *Wall Street Journal,* September 9, 2014, http://online.wsj.com/articles/amid-kale-and-quinoa-pop-tarts-keep-hanging-on-1410305326.

Anne Steib, "Interview with Nature's Path Foods' Arjan Stephens," *Examiner.com,* August 17, 2009, http://www.examiner.com/article/interview-with-nature-s-path-foods-arjan-stephens.

"Arjan Stephens: Growing An Organic Legacy," Two Birds Apparel blog, March 31, 2014, http://www.twobirdsapparel.com/blogs/lifestyle/13274749-arjan-stephens-growing-an-organic-legacy.

"Talking Shop with…Arjan Stephens," GroceryHeadquarters.com, http://www.groceryheadquarters.com/2011/10/talking_shop_with_arjan_stephens/.

"Whole Foods and Nature's Path Team up to Fight Poverty," *Progressive Grocer,* February 24, 2011, http://www.progressivegrocer.com/whole-foods-and-natures-path-team-fight-poverty.

Max Goldberg, "GMO OMG is an Important Movie That Every Person Needs to See," Living Maxwell website, September 26, 2013, http://livingmaxwell.com/gmo-omg-movie-review.

Waylon Lewis, "Independent Family-Owned Nature's Path is Doing the Right Thing and Having Fun Doing So," *Elephant Journal,* April 17, 2013, http://www.elephantjournal.com/2013/04/independent-family-owned-natures-path-is-doing-the-right-thing-having-fun-doing-so/.

"Talking to Nature's Path at Natural Products Expo West," 2012, http://www.youtube.com/watch?v=DiNC11q-JrI.

Press release, "Nature's Path Plants it Forward With Gardens for Good Grant Program," http://www.prnewswire.com/news-releases/natures-path-plants-it-forward-with-gardens-for-good-grant-program-149634635.html.

Weldon Burge, "Out of the Office," *Organic Gardening,* April/May 2011. 60–63.

Arjan Stephens featured in *Business in Vancouver,* December 16, 2012, http://www.biv.com/article/2012/12/arjan-stephens/.

Kathryn Engel, "A Canadian Global Success Story Eyes Up Breakfast Food Lovers Across the Pond," *Slick World,* January/February 2010. 60–64.

Bruce Boyers, "Following Nature's Path," *Organic Connections*, January–February 2013. 4–7.

Steve Burgess, "Nature's Path: Food For Thought," *Nuvo,* Autumn 2013. 84–88.

Robin Roberts, "Ratana Stephens: A Natural Path to Riches," *Mehfil,* December/January 2010. 42–46.

Deanna Rosolen, "Nature's Path Foods Stewardship Award," *Food in Canada,* 2014. 32–33.

Appendix

Thierry Vrain, "A Round Up Ready World." Paper presented at International Horticulture Society conference in August 2014 in Brisbane, Australia. To be published in *Acta Horticulturae* in 2015.

Gurdeep Stephens, "GMOs by Nation," The Deeper Side blog, December 2013, http://thedeepersideblog.com/2013/12/09/gmos-by-nation/.

John Fagan, Michael Antoniou and Claire Robinson, "GMO Myths and Truths," http://earthopensource.org/index.php/reports/gmo-myths -and-truths.

Canadian Biotechnology Action Network report, "Will GM Crops Feed the World?," October 2014, cban.ca/Resources/Topics/Feeding-the-World.

Permaculture Research Institute, "UN: Only Small Farmers and Agro-ecology Can Feed the World," September 26, 2014, http://perma-culturenews.org/2014/09/26/un-small-farmers-agroecology-can -feed-world/.

European Network of Scientists for Social and Environmental Responsibility, "Statement: No scientific consesnsus on GMO safety," October 21, 2013, http://www.ensser.org/increasing-public-information/ no-scientific-consensus-on-gmo-safety/.

PHOTO CREDITS

Apart from the stock photo on pages 30–31, every photo in this book directly relates to Nature's Path gardens, our history and/or our valued team members. The bulk of the farm photos come from our family farms in Saskatchewan and Montana. Several of the other farm photos come from Dag Falck, our Organic Programs Manager. Jyoti took some photos at our farm partners in Brazil. Plants and flowers shown in the book are all touched by our hands, being from our gardens (mine, Richmond home office, Dag's, Arran and Ratana's, and Arjan's gardens). Rimjhim took many of the beautiful photos from the family gardens as did various team members. Where possible, the photographers are credited below. Some of my favourite photos are from a recent trip to the restored Schulenberg Prairie at the Morton Arboretum. Except for a couple of magazine covers and the photos of hemp, all the other images not credited belong to the Stephens family and the Nature's Path and Manna archives.

Gurdeep Stephens: pages i, iv, xv, 24, 25, 90 (top right), 91 (right), 93 (top right and bottom), 101 (left), 106, 109 (right), 118 (left and right), 122 (top), 123 (top), 124, 125, 130 (left), 133 (right), 141 (top left), 147 (all), 159, 160 (bottom), 168 (left), 169, 170, 173 (right), 175.

Keith Moulding: pages ii, xii, xxii–1, 33 (all), 38 (top right), 41, 44, 45, 48, 49, 50 (right), 84–85, 86, 107, 114 (right), 115 (all), 122 (bottom and top right), 126–127, 132 (left), 150 (bottom), 171 (right), 184 (left), 189.

Rimjhim Duggal Stephens: pages vi, viii, xiv, 20, 28 (top left and right), 52 (all), 53 (all), 56 (left), 89 (right), 94, 95, 102 (left), 109 (left), 117, 131 (left), 142, 148, 172 (right), 184 (right).

Noel Hendrickson: pages ix, x, 32, 34, 88 (all), 89 (left), 91 (left), 97, 98 (all), 100, 102 (right), 110, 143, 157 (left), 166, 171 (left), 185.

John and Ocean Robbins: page xiii.

Arran Stephens: pages 11 (right), 12 (right), 14 (bottom), 23 (all), 26 (right), 28 (bottom left), 38 (top left and bottom), 55 (all), 112 (right), 130 (right), 138 (left), 165, 174.

Suzanne Soldan: page 15.

Dag Falck: pages 21, 46–47, 51, 58, 60, 71 (all), 73, 78, 80, 92, 96, 103, 114 (left), 128, 132 (right), 139 (left), 144, 160 (top), 163, 164, 173 (left).

Stock photo: pages 30–31.

Horizon Air: page 50 (left).

David Suzuki Foundation: page 67.

Arlen Redkop/*Vancouver Sun*: page 68.

Ken McCormick: pages 69, 70 (top right).

Nicolette Mahoney: pages 83, 138 (right), 140 (left), 197 (right).

Jyoti Stephens: pages 167, 168 (right).

Shanti Stephens Schramm: page 101 (right).

Hemp Oil Canada: pages 104, 105.

Robyn O'Brien: page 108.

Markus Schramm: page 111 (right).

Kaitlyn McQuaid: page 117 (left).

Christian Schramm: page 117 (right).

Biancha Klimp: page 123 (bottom).

Brent Flink: page 131 (right).

Jeff Deweerd: page 133 (left).

Shannon Chadwick: pages 139 (right), 141 (bottom left).

Sherry Sweetapple: page 140 (right).

Guy Manwaring: page 145.

Vilicus Farms: pages 151, 152 (all).

Darcy Smith: page 153.

Ellie Falzone: page 155 (top).

Rachel Bailey: pages 155 (bottom), 156, 158 (left).

Bill Picha: page 157 (right).

Gemma Gibs: page 158 (right).

Pascal Courty: page 172 (left).

Tessa Lloyd: page 201.

INDEX

Page numbers in *italics* refer to image captions, or, where captions are absent, to images. Some images have not been individually identified when they appear on pages or within page ranges otherwise listed.

ABOUT THE AUTHOR

Gurdeep Stephens is the second daughter of Nature's Path co-founders Arran and Ratana Stephens and sister to Shanti, Jyoti and Arjan. Gurdeep has lived in five countries, speaks as many languages, has a Masters in Biopsychology and started a PhD in Developmental Neurobiology. A singer and writer, Gurdeep is on the advisory council of the University of Victoria's School of Environmental Studies. Working in her family's businesses, Gurdeep has been a carrot peeler, bus-girl, order picker, waitress, cashier, go-fer, export sales manager, blogger and special projects manager. She returned from 13 years in Europe in 2009 and settled on the Pacific West Coast with her economist husband of 20 years and their two children. Gurdeep is passionate about Earth honouring and food security. *This Earth Is Ours* is her second book.

ISBN 978-0-9938521-1-4

Edited and proofread by Marial Shea
Index by Lana Okerlund
Cover design, layout and typesetting by Jeff Deweerd
Painting on cover by Arran Stephens
Cover painting photographed by Rachel Topham
Interior page design, layout and typesetting by Jan Westendorp,
Kato Design and Photo

Printed in Canada by Friesens

Printed on Forest Stewardship Council (FSC) certified paper, which is acid free, ancient-forest friendly and has been processed without chlorine. The paper contains a minimum of 10 percent post-consumer recycled content and all the inks are vegetable based.

Published by D&I Enterprises, Victoria, BC

Nature's Path is and always will be a part of my family. They have been there with me celebrating my wedding and the birth of my dau
110%. Happy Anniversary. —**Laura** ¶ When I left university, I wanted to go out and make a difference in the world. I dabbled in po
courageously proactive solution to so many of society's problems is phenomenal motivation to get up and go to work every day. Who
incredibly excited for the progress yet to come. —**Kyla** ¶ I feel incredibly blessed to be a part of this wonderful company and the larger
only is Nature's Path making a real impact on the food choices people make everyday but they are contributing to a more sustainable
people involved in this shift forward, by the dedication and the pioneering of the family in this flourishing industry and by their courag
Manager at PricewaterhouseCooper. Nature's Path immediately became my favourite client, the kind of client that's on your mind all t
Saskatchewan, my parents instilled in me at an early age the desire to give back, to be environmentally friendly and sustainable, and to
left PricewaterhouseCooper, it would be to Nature's Path and throughout my career I used Nature's Path as my role model busines
I jumped at it. It's a weird feeling, but Nature's Path feels like home and I am incredibly honoured to be able to work with such talented
With two young children, I want the best for them including what they eat—they are so incredibly proud that their Mom works at Nat
and family it seems like the logical beginning of my passion. Majoring in marketing, it was a challenge to fulfill my blooming passion
in Singapore. When I started working for Nature's Path I innocently thought, "Great, I get to work with food, this will be fun." ¶ After c
Nature's Path is family-run and I already feel like part of the family! I think that it's amazing that a huge company can still feel someh
me more aware of my community, what I put into my body, and how my work will impact the future generations. What started out inno
I served at Que Pasa (20 years to be precise), but to have the privilege to join this team and work for this family is like the icing on t
teammates, to picking berries in the garden, to having an ethical and balanced way of providing for my children—it's like I've been pl
found it," it truly resonated with me. Ultimately, I want to be proud of where I work and what I do, and to me that means doing good
Path. We're truly leaving a legacy of positivity and hope for future generations—one uniting mission for all team members at Nature's
other growing young companies committed to delivering excellent product. But as soon as I arrived at Nature's Path, and had the priv
to live my life. ¶ Working with the family in the company's organic garden, learning the importance of leaving the earth better than wher
Working with knowledgeable team members, walking the floors of the factory, sharing our products at numerous events I came to app
double digit growth on a consistent basis. It was wonderful, crazy and sometimes dizzying—never dull and always thrilling. I was able
introduction of a superfood, our first time on national TV, tremendous expansion at grocery and championing legislation for GMO lab
cereals in North America. Being part of a company that experiences explosive growth means you get to wear many hats, take on new re
that we know made a difference in people's lives and being committed as a sustainable and socially responsible company. ¶ I am grate
the team members I worked with, the lasting friendships I made and most of all—the proud and active role we played as a compan
support mandatory labeling and our underwriting of the marvelous and must-see movie, GMO OMG, were truly some of the proudes
sure social responsibility was an integral part of everything we did. Through our various philanthropic programs, we gave back millions
to build a strong marketing infrastructure, help develop our brand management system and bring in partners to help add resources. Th
other, the team and business, kept all of us going the extra mile to keep up with the growing demand for our products. My